Carving Flora
& Fables in *Wood*

E. J. Tange

Sterling Publishing C New York

Oak Tree Press Co., Ltd London & Sydney

Other books by E. J. Tangerman

Carving Faces and Figures in Wood
Carving Religious Motifs in Wood
Carving Wooden Animals

Library of Congress Cataloging in Publication Data
Tangerman, E. J. (Elmer John), 1907–
    Carving flora and fables in wood.
    Includes index.
    1. Wood-carving—Technique.   2. Design, Decora-
tive—Plant forms.   3. Fables in art.   I. Title.
TT199.7.T334   736'.4   80-54336
ISBN 0-8069-8982-3 (pbk.)   AACR2
Oak Tree ISBN 7061-8982-3

Copyright © 1981 by Sterling Publishing Co., Inc.
Two Park Avenue, New York, N.Y. 10016
Distributed in Australia by Oak Tree Press Co., Ltd.
P.O. Box J34, Brickfield Hill, Sydney 2000, N.S.W.
Distributed in the United Kingdom by Oak Tree Press Ltd. U.K.
Available in Canada from Oak Tree Press Ltd.
% Canadian Manda Group, 215 Lakeshore Boulevard East
Toronto, Ontario M5A 3W9
Manufactured in the United States of America

Contents

Fig. 1. This one-piece daisy is a variation of the old whittling trick—the fan. It is cut across grain so that the petals can later be split and spread. In this case, the petals were not interlocked, but held in place with thread. See Chapter III.

Why Carve Flora and Fables?

THE ANSWER TO THAT QUESTION is that, sooner or later, everybody does. Foliage and fanciful figures—especially gods and heroes—were popular subjects for ancient carvers. The Egyptians, for example, were partial to the lotus and to creatures—like the Sphinx—that combined the attributes of various species; the Greeks favored the acanthus and their gods; Europeans carved the oak, the grape, folk heroes like William Tell or Charlemagne, the griffin, and the dragon; China and Japan carved dragons, vines, and water lilies; the Norsemen doted on strange animals and gods; the Germans and Dutch were masters of high-relief forest scenes.

The situation hasn't changed much. American carvers try Paul Bunyan, Babe Ruth, Abraham Lincoln, or the current president, and carvers in Bali, Japan, China, Africa and other faraway places still incorporate foliage, gods and heroes, as well as fanciful creatures into their work. One reason is that foliage, with fabulous figures interspersed, is an interesting and infinitely variable way of decorating a surface or tying together elements of an in-the-round composition, or even for providing such utilitarian service as supporting otherwise fragile parts of a figure. Another reason is that foliage and fable are part of the basic fabric of our past; both are pastoral and rural in feeling, rather than sophisticated and urban.

In this book, I have tried to assemble examples of a wide variety of floral and fabulous subjects, while consciously avoiding the trite and familiar examples available elsewhere. They offer fascinating possibilities, among them the pragmatic one that exact portraiture—either of foliage or of mythical heroes—is not required because we don't observe foliage that closely, and authentic portraits of the ancient gods and heroes do not exist. Even a tyro can achieve creditable results.

Many of the pieces shown here are my own originals, sometimes adapted from traditional sources, and sometimes, of necessity, entirely imaginary. For typical designs I have provided step-by-step photographs, with hints for the solution of knotty problems. For most, there are front and side patterns; suggestions for your own designs, for finishing, for wood, tool selection, and for size, are all included as well. The tedious research has been done, leaving the way open for pleasant, fascinating and rewarding carving. I wish you well.

E. J. TANGERMAN

CHAPTER I

A Primer on Woods

THE WOOD YOU CHOOSE may depend upon what is available and what you are willing to pay. Many carvers salvage wood from old furniture, fallen trees, or from the shores of streams, lakes or oceans. If you have a choice, ask yourself what is the natural color of the bird or animal you plan to carve? What tools do you plan to use? Is the carving to be painted, textured, polished? Where will it be used or displayed?

As you can see, one question leads to another when you select a wood. If you are a beginner or a figure whittler, the best wood is probably basswood (also called "bee tree"). It is soft, colorless, easy to carve, and hasn't much tendency to split. Ponderosa pine is almost as good, if you avoid the strongly colored pieces. Sugar pine, commonly called "white pine," is a bit more porous, but also very good. Jelutong, a recent import from Indonesia, is like basswood. All take color well, but are too soft to wear well or carry much detail.

Other available soft woods are poplar, which bruises easily and tends to grip tools, so is hard to cut; cedar, which is easy to cut but has a distinctive color; willow, which has a tendency to split; and cypress, which does not wear well. Spanish cedar, once familiar in cigar boxes, is a common carving wood in Mexico.

Many American whittlers have used local woods, particularly the fruit and nut woods. All are harder than those previously mentioned and have a tendency to check in large pieces, but they will take more detail and undercutting, give a better finish, and all have interesting color. Among these are pear, pecan, cherry, apple, and black walnut. The last mentioned is probably the best American carving wood. It has a fine, tough grain, takes detail and undercuts, finishes beautifully, but is inherently dark when oiled (it can be bleached with oxalic acid). The mountain-grown Eastern white oaks are hard to carve, but can take detail and are inherently strong. Avoid swamp or red oak, which has a very prominent grain and is coarse in structure. (Oak has a bad reputation because of the cheap "fumed oak" furniture that once was found everywhere, but it can be darkened with concentrated ammonia, or walnut-stained.) Dogwood is very hard and withstands shock (hence its use in handles), but it tends to check.

Where they are available, butternut, red alder, and myrtle are good for carving, particularly the first two. Redwood (sequoia) is durable, but some pieces have alternating hard and soft grain that causes trouble. Sweet or red gum (also called American satinwood) is more durable and uniform than cedar but tends to warp and twist. Beech, hickory, sycamore, and magnolia are hard to cut and are good only for shallow carving. Ash is stringy, but can support considerable detail. Birch is somewhat like hard, rock, or sugar maple—durable, but hard to carve and finish. Many suppliers have soft maple, but it is not a good carving wood. In the Southwest, there are mesquite, ironwood, and osage orange, all very hard, inclined to split, and difficult to carve, but capable of fine finishes. Mesquite, like our fruit woods, is subject to insect attack. Holly, our whitest wood, is usually available only in small pieces; it is hard and tends to check.

Among imported woods, the most familiar is mahogany, which is not one wood but many, with quality and color (pinkish white to red-brown) depending upon source and individual piece. Some, like Honduras, are fine-grained, even though relatively soft. Cuban mahogany is dense and varies in hardness; South American varieties tend to be grainy and splinter easily; Philippine mahogany, commonly available, tends to be coarse in grain, but I have six samples which range from white to dark red in color and from coarse to dense in grain. There are also other woods now being sold as mahogany, like luanda and primavera, a white wood that cuts like mahogany and can be stained to look exactly like it. (Mahogany, by the way, when sanded makes a very fine dust which travels all through the house.)

My favorite carving wood is Thai or Burmese teak, which doesn't rot. is not subject to insect attack, and does not warp or check to any degree. It is an excellent carving wood that will support considerable detail, but it does have a tendency to dull tools rapidly despite its inherent oil. The dulling is probably a result of silica soaked up from the marshy land on which it grows. Chinese teak is red and harsh-grained, so the Chinese stained or painted it black—hence the common opinion that teak is black. It is actually light green when cut, and finishes to a medium reddish-brown, sometimes with slight graining. Another good wood is English sycamore, or harewood, which is about as white as American holly, and is available in wide boards.

Ebony, which comes from Africa, India, Ceylon, Indonesia, and South and Central America, varies in color from a solid black (Gabon from Africa) to dark brown with black striping (Macassar from Indonesia, and Calamander from Ceylon). It is very hard, as are lignum vitae (Africa and Mexico, where it is called *guayacan*) and cocobola (avoid inhaling the dust; it causes lung inflammation). Lacewood, briar, sandal, and satinwood are less hard and will take fine detail. All of these are more suited to carving with tools than with the knife. The same goes for rosewood, which comes from a number of southern countries and varies from soft brown through red and red-brown to purple, with other colors thrown in. This is a beautiful wood, but expensive, and should be reserved for pieces in which the grain and color are not competing with detail. Another fascinating wood is pink ivory from Africa, which is very hard and pinkish to red in color; it is the rarest wood. Other woods like purpleheart, thuya, madrona, greenheart, vermilion and bubinga are also imported and offer a range of colors. All are expensive, hard to find in large or thick pieces, and hard to carve, but they are worth it, occasionally, for their grain.

The variety of woods available is almost endless, and my best advice is to start with the more familiar and less problematic ones, and then to proceed cautiously to the exotic and expensive varieties, testing as you go.

CHAPTER II

The Tools – When and Where

FLORAL AND FOLIAGE ELEMENTS traditionally have been the basis of much formal woodcarving design. Because foliage has so many concave and similarly formed surfaces, specialized woodcarving tools were developed long ago. Simple flowers and fruits can be shaped in the round or in high relief with the knife alone, of course, but such forms as oak, grape and acanthus leaves, bunches of grapes, vines, and complex flowers take shape much faster with chisels.

The principal requirement in any carving is a good knife made of carbon rather than stainless steel, so that it will hold an edge. If it is a pocketknife, it should have two or, at most, three blades and be free of can openers, cork-screws, and clips, all of which can bruise the hand during extensive use. I carry two pocketknives, both small; one has three blades, pen, spear and B-clip (*B*, Fig. 2), and the other is a penknife with pen and B-clip. This provides variety in point size, shape, and strength.

When I'm at home, I frequently use fixed-blade knives, which are safer and easier on the hand because of the larger, more comfortable handles. I have some equipped with chucks to take replaceable blades. If you use the latter, make sure the chuck is sturdy enough to grip securely (keep it supertight!) and that the blades are thick enough to be stiff; some commercial handles are suited only to cut balsa and linoleum blocks. In replaceable blades, I prefer a modified B-clip and a thin concave "hook" blade designed originally for working leather. Avoid knives with elaborate handles; they are not versatile and are difficult to handle.

For most work, a blade length of 1½ in (4 cm) or less is advisable; longer blades tend to bend, catch near the heel, and are difficult to control when you cut with the tip. The wider the blade, the straighter and more stable your cuts, but the greater the difficulty in cutting concave areas and in tight places. If you are delighted by heavy chips and big cuts, you'll break the

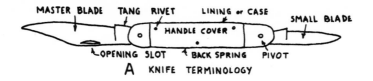

MASTER BLADE   TANG   RIVET   LINING or CASE   SMALL BLADE
HANDLE COVER
OPENING SLOT   BACK SPRING   PIVOT
A   KNIFE   TERMINOLOGY

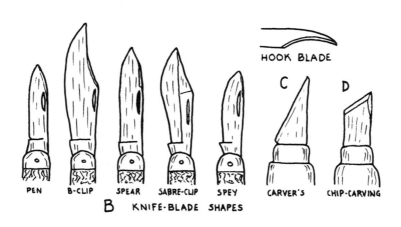

HOOK BLADE

C   D

PEN   B-CLIP   SPEAR   SABRE-CLIP   SPEY   CARVER'S   CHIP-CARVING

B   KNIFE-BLADE   SHAPES

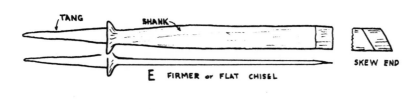

TANG   SHANK

SKEW END

E   FIRMER or FLAT CHISEL

F   SHANK SHAPES

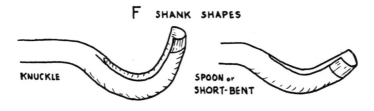

KNUCKLE   SPOON or SHORT-BENT

Fig. 2.

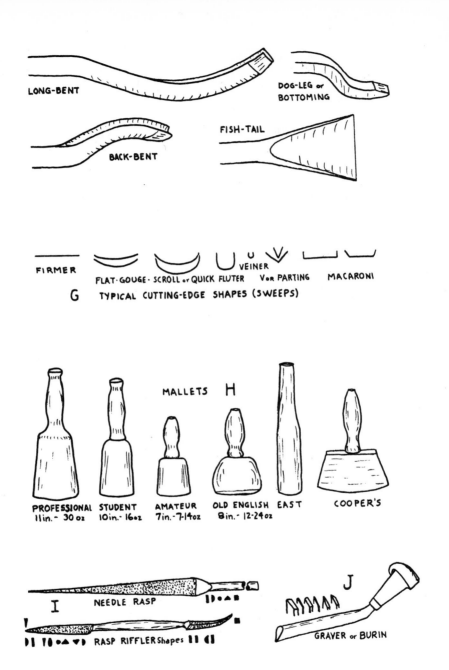

LONG-BENT

DOG-LEG or BOTTOMING

BACK-BENT

FISH-TAIL

FIRMER   FLAT·GOUGE· SCROLL or QUICK FLUTER   VEINER   V or PARTING   MACARONI

G   TYPICAL CUTTING-EDGE SHAPES (SWEEPS)

MALLETS   H

PROFESSIONAL   STUDENT   AMATEUR   OLD ENGLISH   EAST   COOPER'S
11 in. - 30 oz   10 in. - 16 oz   7 in. - 7-14 oz   8 in. - 12-24 oz

I   NEEDLE RASP

RASP RIFFLER Shapes

J

GRAVER or BURIN

Fig. 3.

11

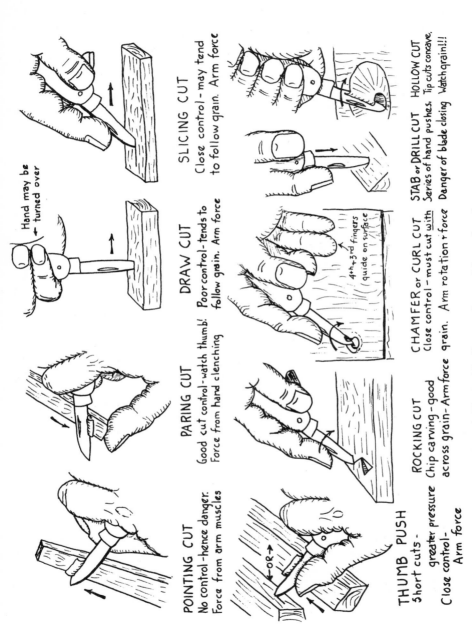

POINTING CUT
No control – hence danger.
Force from arm muscles

PARING CUT
Good cut control – watch thumb!
Force from hand clenching

Hand may be turned over

DRAW CUT
Poor control – tends to
follow grain. Arm force

SLICING CUT
Close control – may tend
to follow grain. Arm force

THUMB PUSH
Short cuts –
greater pressure
Close control –
Arm force

ROCKING CUT
Chip carving – good
across grain – Arm force

CHAMFER or CURL CUT
Close control – must cut with
grain. Arm rotation + force

4th + 3rd fingers
guide on surface

STAB or DRILL CUT
Series of hand pushes.
Danger of blade closing

HOLLOW CUT
Tip cuts concave.
Watch grain!!

Fig. 4. Typical knife cuts done with one hand.

12

narrow blades. I should warn you that you should *cut out* chips, not try to wedge them out—that's likely to break both wood and knife.

It is, of course, possible to make your own special knives as many whittlers do. They're usually special-purpose to get into particular spots and for the repetitive carving of a particular shape. Such knives are made from slivers of safety-razor blades bound into dowel handles, reground straight razors, or other pieces of good and tempered steel. The principal cautions here are to grind very slowly to avoid burning the cutting edge, and to bind the blade securely into the handle. A blade that wobbles or tends to snap closed is likely to cut you rather than the wood.

Knives should be kept very sharp; this reduces the effort required, avoids tearing and splitting to a degree, and gives smoother cuts and better control. A fine-grained stone and a leather strop are helpful—they should be all that is needed unless you nick or break the blade. The most common cut in whittling is one similar to paring a potato, in which the ball of the thumb is in the path of the blade. It may be advisable to wear a finger stall of leather or rubber on the thumb—stationery stores sell them in rubber for people who sort papers. A Band-Aid or tape on the middle joint of your index finger will be helpful as well; it prevents blisters if you haven't built up a callous there.

When you whittle, you must keep your mind on what you're doing; you can't watch TV or converse. Many whittlers have remarked that they only cut themselves when they're demonstrating or teaching, because they talk when they should be intent on carving. Learn to be careful with the knife. Don't stick the blade into the wood in such a way that the blade may close. Always close the blade with the palm of the hand while you hold the knife in the fingertips of the other. Don't have two blades open at once, even for sharpening. If the blade has no boss, be especially careful to keep your fingers from slipping down onto the sharp edge. Don't hammer the blade, and don't use it to cut newspaper clippings, pare your fingernails, or strip insulation from wire—all are hard on it.

A knife or razor has a feather edge when it is sharp; highly magnified, the blade will be seen as a series of tiny sawteeth extending both ways from center. Honing removes the hairy feathers and reduces the size of the teeth, and stropping aligns them temporarily. Cutting bends the edge teeth out of line and requires re-stropping. My experience is that softer woods require a sharper edge to cut cleanly; too fine an edge on a knife when cutting ebony or ivory will break down too quickly. Actually, I find that I need a better edge on a knife than I do on a chisel, perhaps largely because I usually use a mallet with the chisels and am not so conscious of the control necessary with a tool that requires more force as it dulls.

Whittling and woodcarving are both paring operations, but whittling implies the use of only one tool (usually the knife) while woodcarving permits the use of many. Also, whittling is usually done on relatively small pieces that can be held in the hand, while woodcarvings often must be secured mechanically in some way. Also, there is a tradition that a whittling is only one piece of wood, while a woodcarving is frequently built up of laminated planks (to avoid checking), or with separate arms and legs or other extensions added later, either to attain favorable grain structure, to simplify carving, or, in these inflationary days, to save wood.

The woodcarver uses flat and curved chisels, just as a carpenter does, but woodcarving chisels are thinner and lighter than carpenter's chisels, come in many more shapes, and are sharpened differently. The basic flat chisel is called a *firmer*, and is sharpened from both sides, so it can be used with either hand, either side up, without gouging into the surface of the piece. It usually has a larger bevel (less included angle) than a carpenter's chisel, although pros adapt the included angle to the hardness of the wood they're cutting.

Firmers are available in width from about ¹⁄₁₆ in (1.6 mm) to 2½ in (4 cm) or so. The curved chisels called *gouges* (see *E, F, G*, Figs. 2 and 3) range from U-shaped to almost flat, and from ¹⁄₁₆ in (1.6 mm) to about 2½ in (4 cm) wide at the cutting edge. The smallest U-shaped gouge is called a *veiner* and, as its name implies, it is used for cutting small grooves, for defining hair, and for very fine detail. A slightly larger one is called a *fluter*— again a descriptive name. The very large ones are used primarily for cutting away waste wood and for rough shaping, although they also serve for finishing large surfaces.

The *parting* or *V-tool* cuts two opposite surfaces simultaneously. It is shaped like a V and is used for outlining, grooving, and many other jobs. It is the most difficult of chisels to sharpen and one of the most difficult to master for cross-grain cutting. Another tool, the *macaroni*, cuts a trench with flat bottom and right-angle or outwardly sloping sides. (A variant, the *fluteroni*, also cuts a trench, but with arcuate corners.) These are rarely used and not included in most tool sets. There is also a common variant of the firmer, the *skew chisel*, in which the cutting edge is at an angle to the axis of the tool, thus providing a point for getting into corners and around surfaces. It is a versatile tool, as is the *bullnose*—a firmer with the cutting edge ground into an arc.

14

Wide tools, and some narrower ones, are tapered down toward the *tang*—which is that portion of the tool driven into the handle. These are called *spade* or *fishtail* tools, and are very helpful for getting into tight places or helping the carver to see what he is doing. The *shank* of a tool behind the cutting edge may also be forged into a curve so that the cutting edge will be able to work in a confined place, such as a concave surface or around a curve. Depending upon the arc of shank curvature, such a tool is called *long-bent* or *short-bent*. Normally the arc is concave (viewed from the top), but it may be convex to handle a specific job, such as forming the surfaces of individual grapes in a bunch or cutting a special shape under an overhang; it is then called a *back-bent* tool. These tools are harder to use than straight ones because of the spring in the bend, and they are more difficult to sharpen.

Carving tools require two hands, except those tools which are very short or specialized, like Japanese tools, which have long, thin handles and short blades. The standard tool is gripped and pushed by one hand, while the other hand guides the tool and keeps it from over-running or following a sudden split or breakout. This creates somewhat of a paradox, because the two hands work against each other. I have not identified which hand does what, because the tools are interchangeable and because the skilled carver learns to hold the tool with either hand to suit the cut. This avoids a lot of moving or altering the position of the work.

With hardwoods, the chisel is held in one hand and struck with the other, making it necessary to support the work in some way. Oriental carvers, who customarily squat cross-legged and mostly carve pieces 1 to 2 ft (30.5 to 61 cm) in length, simply wedge the work into their laps. (Their chisels often have no handles; their mallets are clubs.) Large panels and large 3 D carvings, unless they are top-heavy, usually require no holding unless very large chisels or mallets are used. The clamping method can suit the piece and be as simple as a nail or two driven through waste wood into a bench or board, or only a vise. Decoy carvers, who turn the piece a great deal, use a special vise with a ball-and-socket swivel that can be clamped at a variety of angles. Another ancient device is the *carver's screw*, which is a long screw put through a hole in the bench or easel and screwed into the bottom of the work, then tightened under the bench with a wing nut. For small panels, a *bench hook* or *bench plate* (see Fig. 5) is portable, convenient, and easy to construct.

For work in harder woods, and for greater precision, it is advisable to use a carver's mallet, which is simply some form of soft-faced hammer. The chisel is held in one hand and the mallet in the other, so extraneous holding is still required. The traditional mallet is like an old-fashioned, wooden potato masher, but it can have a flat face like a cooper's hammer, or it can be simply a club with a handle whittled at one end. Modern carvers have developed many kinds of mallets, some with plastic faces to reduce the noise, possible handle splintering, and shock to the driving arm, some with lead or copper replacing the wooden head, some even made out of old washing-machine wringer rolls. This is a matter of individual selection. I have half-a-dozen mallets of various kinds, ranging from light to heavy, because I work principally in hardwoods and use a light mallet even for most small cuts. With the mallet, I can control the force behind the cutting edge much more accurately than I can with just an arm push.

Carving tools are sized by the width of the cutting edge, ranging from ¹⁄₁₆ in (1.6 mm) to ⅜ in (9.5 mm) in sixteenths, up to 1 in (25.4 mm) in eighths, and in larger steps up to the maximum, usually around 2½ in (6 cm) for flat gouges. European tools are sized in millimeters: 1, 2, 3, 4, 5, 6, 7, 8, 10, 12, 16, 20, 25, 30, 35, etc. (1 mm = 0.037 in). The gouges are also often numbered by the "London system" which measures the arc or radius of the sweep. A firmer is No. 1; a skew firmer, 2; a quite-flat gouge, 3; and a U-shaped one, 11 or 12, with the other arcs in between.

There are also many auxiliary tools, like straight and coping saws, rasps and riffler files (1, Fig. 3), scrapers, hand routers, and the usual carpenter's tools. (I use carpenter's chisels and gouges for roughing; they're heavier and cheaper.) Of these, the riffler files, which come in various shapes and sizes—some straight, some bent, with different surfaces at each end—are convenient for finishing in tight spots, over knots and faults, and on very small work.

In some instances, you may have a choice of handle on the chisels. Usual handles are round or octagonal, tapering toward the cutting edge. Round ones are made of maple, ash, beech or boxwood; the octagonal ones may even be dogwood (which is preferred in Oberammergau). Octagonal handles are less likely to turn in your hand or to roll on a bench. (There are now some plastic handles as well, of course.) My preference is for octagonal wood handles, with a brass ferrule at the tang to prevent splitting under mallet blows.

The customary way to carve is standing up at a bench that is heavy enough so it won't shift. Sculptors who work on large blocks prefer a four-legged stand weighted at the base with a rock, so they can move around it. Some have lazy-Susan (rotating) tops and height adjustments. Cuckoo-clock carvers

16

have tables with heavy, sloping tops. I often work at an outdoor trestle table or indoors on a card table, and I sit down whenever possible. The main thing is to have a stable surface which will absorb mallet blows, plus a level surface on which tools not in use may be placed. My experience is that this will be a relatively small number at any given time, so an elaborate rack of tools at the back of the bench is not necessary. It goes without saying that good lighting is a must, particularly when dark woods like walnut are being carved, and that adequate ventilation is helpful. All of these things are matters of individual preference, and depend also on the size and complexity of the work. You don't *need* a studio unless you teach or want to create an atmosphere.

As would be expected, we have mechanized woodcarving as far as possible. Circular saws and bandsaws help shape blanks; routers cut away backgrounds; coping saws, power drills and sanders are also used. Carvers of totem poles and wooden Indians and other heroic figures have adopted the chain saw— with a great gain in speed of cutting but a great potential for making the user deaf and driving his or her neighbors insane. Carvers of small objects and/or very hard materials use hand grinders or flexible-shaft machines with shaped cutters, and claim extraordinary results with them. Some have even adopted dental drills. My experience is that they are hard to control, chew rather than cut the wood, and throw dust and chips over a considerable area, so the user needs safety glasses. I have even met a few carvers who use pneumatic or electric hammers with fitted chisels. Like the profiler and duplicator, such equipment is primarily commercial. It may save time and effort in some instances, but hand finishing is usually required anyway if the surfaces are to have any quality.

You don't need nearly as many tools as you or a tool salesman may think. They should be selected to suit your ability and your customary subject. In several cases in this book, I have listed the tools I used for a particular project. I find that I seem to average only about a dozen tools, even for the most complex subject, and some of these are conveniences rather than necessities. To a considerable degree, a design or carving should be adapted to your skill and your tools. The tendency is to have tools that are too large because they remove wood faster. Balinese carvers, who are currently making some of the finest and most delicate sculptures, have only a few small tools and almost no auxiliary equipment, as I have pointed out previously, but then they don't worship time as we do.

Even the authorities disagree on the proper kit for a beginner. Commercial suppliers offer kits with considerable variety, undoubtedly based on the recommendation of some particular carver. Charles M. Sayers, who taught panel carving in particular, suggested four tools with which to start: ½-in (12.7-mm) No. 39 parting tool—or ⅜ in (9.6 mm), or ⅝ in (16 mm); ⅝-in (16-mm) No. 5 straight gouge; 1-in (25.4-mm) No. 3—or ⅞-in (22.4-mm)—straight gouge; and ⅜-in (9.6-mm) No. 7 straight gouge. For relief carving, he added a ⅜-in (9.6-mm) No. 3 straight gouge. H. M. Sutter, who has taught carving to a great many people during the past 30 years, starts his students with five tools, plus an all-purpose carver's knife: a ⅜-in (9.6-mm) No. 3 straight gouge; ⅝-in (16-mm) No. 5 straight gouge (these two preferably fishtail); ⅜-in (9.6-mm) No. 9 straight gouge; a 1-mm or ¹⁄₃₂-in No. 11 veiner; and a ⅜-in (9.6-mm) No. 41 parting tool. Note that neither one suggests fancy shapes or skew chisels—at least to start.

My best advice is to start small, with the aid of a capable carver (if possible) and a clear understanding of the kind of work you wish to do. Many carvers, and some teachers, make their own tools as they find a need for them, grinding tempered steel to suit, or forging the tool and finding someone locally to do the tempering. You'll need at least a flat gouge for roughing, shaping and cleaning up; a firmer for finishing and flat surfaces; a veiner for outlining and emphasizing lines; and a V-tool for outlining square corners and square-bottom grooves. A gouge or two with different sweeps and, probably, a skew chisel are the first additions, followed by gouges and firmers of different widths. A good rule may be adapted from that suggested to amateur photographers when they add lenses: When you get additional tools of approximately the same shape or sweep, double or halve the previous dimension. Thus, if you have a ½-in (12.7-mm) No. 5 gouge and want another of the same sweep, get a ¼-in (6.3-mm) or a 1-in (25.4-mm), unless you have continued need for one closer to ½ in (12.7 mm). The same rule might be applied to supplementing sweeps; if you have No. 3, you don't need No. 4 or 5—go to No. 6 or even No. 9.

Actual carving with chisels is, for me, much less complex than carving with a knife, because the individual tool is less versatile unless it is gripped in the fingertips and used like a knife. There *are* a few fundamentals. Because the tool is pushed by arm power on soft woods, it must be restrained by the opposite hand to keep it from cutting too far, a problem which is minimized when a mallet is used. (I have never been an advocate of driving a chisel with the heel of the hand. I've known several carvers who irreparably damaged their hands that way.) If you are not familiar with hammering a nail or a chisel, you must learn to watch the cutting tip, not the chisel head. The potato-masher mallet is a help in this because it reduces the necessity of hitting the chisel head exactly square. Obviously, the angle with which the chisel is struck or pushed influences the direction of the cut.

As cutting begins, you must adjust the angle of the tool so it cuts through the wood at the desired level; too high an angle will cause it to cut deeper and deeper; too shallow an angle will cause it to run out. This is particularly important with the high-sweep or U-shaped gouges: If the cut is too deep, the edges of the gouge can get below the wood surface and tear the fibres. When cuts are started, it is advisable to start at the edge when possible, because if you cut to an edge, the chisel may break out the fibres there rather than cutting through them. In relief cutting, it is important to outline the desired shape by "setting in"—driving the firmer or gouge into the wood to the desired depth along the line, so that cuts made to remove background wood will stop at the cut-line instead of splitting or running into the design. When a chisel is driven vertically into wood, it obviously must wedge the fibres aside, so it will cause crushing and splintering of fibres along the edge of the outline. This can be avoided by cutting a groove just outside the outline with a veiner, fluter or V-tool, so the edge of the groove touches the line. Then, when the firmer or gouge is driven in along the line, the groove provides relief for the wedge at the surface. As a matter of fact, in shallow relief carving, particularly in green wood, it is often possible to get the required depth of background (called "bosting") with a deep fluter alone, leaving the desired small arc at the bottom edge of the upstanding portion.

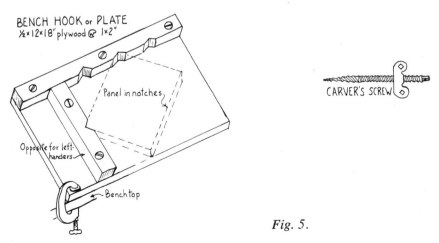

BENCH HOOK or PLATE
½×12×18" plywood @ 1×2"

Panel in notches

Opposite for left-handers

Benchtop

CARVER'S SCREW

Fig. 5.

CHAPTER III

Whittle Simple Flowers

GRINLING GIBBONS WAS NOTED FOR HIS SWAGS OF FLOWERS and leaves in high relief, and many a carver before his time and since has used flower motifs, particularly the rose and the acanthus leaf. Most of these were used in essentially formal carving, and usually were carved in rather high relief. However, many whittlers have also made flowers, some of them as one-piece "tricks"—variations of the puff of curled shavings or the fan. In recent years, the flower produced by multiple shavings has been particularly popular as a demonstration and low-priced commodity at woodcarving shows.

To make a curled-petal flower, the only requirements are wood that shaves well with the grain (like white pine or basswood), a sharp knife, and a good eye. You may prefer to soak the wood in advance, so that the shaving will not split ahead of the knife. All you do is whittle the stick roughly circular, then make thin shavings around and around it until you have the desired number of petals. The individual petal normally should be started on the side rather than the end of the stick so that the petal end is round, and the cuts should be ended at a fixed point set by the first row cut around.

Such a flower can be carved double, or "mum" shape, by running shavings from both directions, but you must take care that the cuts from above and below are kept ¼ in (6.4 mm) or so apart so petals are not split off. It is also possible to carve miniature Christmas trees in this fashion by making a series of collars of shavings, each one with progressively shorter shavings. (That's the way we Boy Scouts also made "fuzz sticks" to act as core tinder when we started a fire.) Once the flower is formed, it can be trimmed to a special shape with scissors, if desired; then the core on the top is cut off and the stub shaped into a dome like a daisy eye, and the bottom is thinned into a fairly thick stem. It is also possible to cut several longer and heavier chips along the stem to suggest leaves. The flower can be colored by spraying or dipping it in dye or vegetable coloring.

Flowers can also be made by sawing or cutting a cross-grained blank in

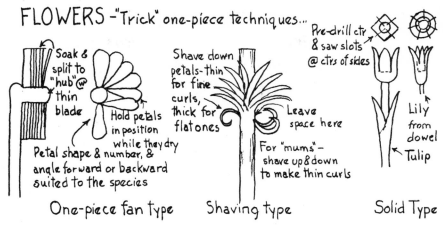

FLOWERS –"Trick" one-piece techniques...

Pre-drill ctr & saw slots @ ctrs of sides

Soak & split to "hub" w̄ thin blade

Hold petals in position while they dry

Petal shape & number, & angle forward or backward suited to the species

One-piece fan type

Shave down petals–thin for fine curls, thick for flat ones

Leave space here

For "mums"– shave up & down to make thin curls

Shaving type

Lily from dowel

Tulip

Solid Type

Fig. 6. Simple flowers made from single pieces of wood. These require wood that can be split or shaved.

... low-relief & in-the-round formal. Various woods

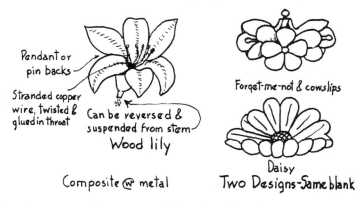

Pendant or pin backs

Stranded copper wire, twisted & glued in throat

Can be reversed & suspended from stem

Wood lily

Composite w̄ metal

Forget-me-not & cowslips

Daisy

Two Designs–Same blank

Fig. 7. Pendants carved from colorful hardwoods. The lily is in vermilion, the other two from the same blank of purpleheart.

soft wood, particularly white pine, and whittling a petal shape both sides of center, then soaking the blank and splitting out a series of thin petals (as shown in Figs. 6, 7, and 8). The petals can be spread and held in a regular fan pattern, or, with a little more difficulty, alternated in direction. If they are held in position until the wood dries, they will stay that way, or they can be held more securely by interlacing them with a colored thread near the outer edge.

21

Fig. 8.

If the blank is for a flower like a daisy, which has the bloom at right angles to the stem, the stem itself must be carved across grain or added later, either of which is a nuisance. However, if the flower is formed parallel to the main stem, as in the violet (Fig. 8), the stem itself can easily be carved later. Again, the petals can be shaped by knife or scissors and the flower-head tinted as desired.

Flowers like the tulip can be carved from the solid blank by drilling a core hole in the end of a stick (of any wood) so that the flat sides are fairly thin, then sawing down in the middle of the flat sides almost to the base of the core hole. Each corner can then be whittled into a petal with a projecting point (Fig. 6), and the leaves and stem carved below the bulbous head.

Somewhat more elaborate and difficult is the carving of flowers for pend-ants and pulls. These can be in the round, of course, or they can be in low relief like those shown (Fig. 7)—either single flowers or groups depending upon the shape desired. I've usually made such flowers in brilliantly colored woods like vermilion, purpleheart, or in a white wood like holly. Flowers are challenging enough so that they deserve a good wood, although they can be made in softer woods if they are to be painted. It's fun to suit the pattern to the available scrap, as I did in the case of the purpleheart carvings (Fig. 7); the blank was over ½ in (12.7 mm) thick, so I could really make two different pendants from the same basic blank.

CHAPTER IV

Start Panel Carving with Flowers

H. M. Sutter's method is relatively fast and easy

STEP-BY-STEP APPRENTICE TRAINING was a teaching method designed for youngsters who had no experience; presently, it has little application except for those who have never used tools. The typical beginner today is an older person with some tool experience—perhaps a great deal—and who wants to get right to carving.

H. M. (Mack) Sutter, of Portland, Oregon, has taught panel carving as well as whittling for more than 40 years, and has developed what is proving to be a highly successful and rapid method of learning. He uses standard-height tables and chairs, the chairs topped by cushions of canvas 5 × 16 × 16 in (12.5 × 40 × 40 cm), stuffed with wood shavings to give a better working height for the carver, and he provides beginner tools kits (see page 18).

Students begin with sharpened and honed tools and work on basswood or jelutong. Beginner designs are all 7 × 8½ in (17.5 × 21 cm) on ¾-in (19-mm) boards, thus the blank can be held conveniently on bench hooks or bench plates of ½-in (12.7-mm) plywood measuring 12 × 18 in (30 × 45 cm) with stopboards screwed in place as shown. Stopboards are notched so the work can be set at an angle if necessary, and some boards are reversed to accommodate left-handed carvers. The bench hook is held to the table edge with a 4-in (10-cm) C-clamp.

The first lesson, surprisingly, is not particularly easy; it requires a great many different types of cuts. It is called the *Eternal Knot*, and the student must work in all directions, so that he or she learns about grain immediately. While the student works, Mack talks about books, woods, patterns, and even demonstrates cutting techniques to an individual or a group as circumstances dictate.

It is quite possible for a deft beginner to teach himself by this method; it is actually the way I learned—except that I had no book for reference until several years later. The virtue of this method is that the individual is immediately challenged and never bored by repetition and tedious detail.

The second panel is the ancient diaper or all-over pattern, for which Mr. Sutter provides only a basic outline. Each individual can work out his or her own detail design; Mack says that no students have ever made exactly the same design. These designs are large and open, so they are basically not difficult to carve in soft wood and can be done with hand pressure alone. Also, the opportunity to vary the design in the second project provides the individual with the opportunity to adjust the intricacy to his own natural ability; he can make something as simple as mounded diamonds or as complex as the pattern in Figure 22. Neither design requires the setting-in or backgrounding that takes added competence, yet either can be shown with pride when completed.

Mack figures that the basic course should consist of about ten 2-hour lessons. However, when a student has tools he can continue carving between lessons, of course, so more material is required. Thus Exercise No. 3, the tulip pattern, is expected to be completed as well. (Figures 12 and 14 are adapted from Designs #26 and #24 of "The Book of Wood Carving," by Charles Marshall Sayers, recently reprinted by Dover Publications, Inc., New York. Exercise #8 is adapted from Sayers' Design #8. They are reproduced here by special permission.)

The intermediate series of lessons begins with Exercise #4, the flower group, and this is the only required panel, because to learn setting-in and bosting, or grounding (cutting away the background), takes some time. However, those who complete #4 may go on to projects of their own or select from #5 the lily, #6 the dogwood, #7 a circular flower group, and #8 a regular design involving precise curves. Again, the middle of #8 can be any of many patterns.

Advanced classes usually undertake individual projects that require specific advice and instruction, or may broaden out into general carving.

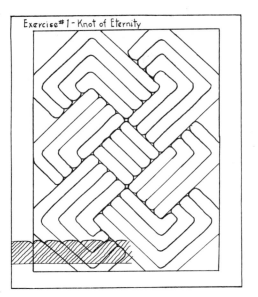

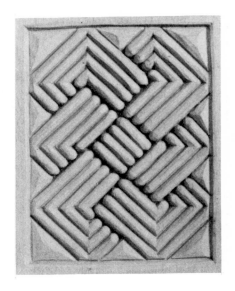

Figs. 9–10. Exercise #1, "the eternal knot," requires cutting across grain and top rounding.

Figs. 11–12. Exercise #2, a diaper pattern, allows for individual variation.

Figs. 13–14. Exercise #3, a stylized tulip, requires a more careful cutting of lines.

Figs. 15–16. Exercise #4, a floral pattern, requires bosting or grounding out.

Figs. 17–18. Exercise #5, a stylized lily, incorporates more intricate detail.

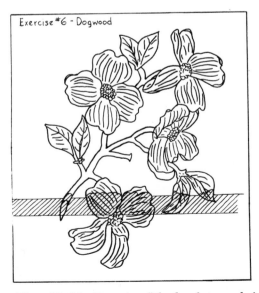

Figs. 19–20. Exercise #6, the dogwood, involves texturing and long, fragile stems.

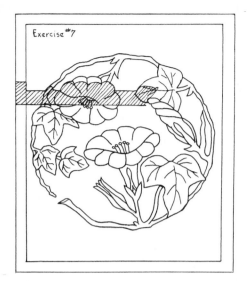

Figs. 21–22. Exercise #7 is a flower group combining previous problems and veining.

Figs. 23–24. Exercise #8 is a traditional pattern of the kind used for door panels.

28

CHAPTER V

Intaglio Carving Is "Inside-Out"

NEARLY A CENTURY AGO, it was quite common to mould designs in relief on the surface of butter, cookies, cakes and gelatine desserts. This was done with moulds of wood which had the design in reverse; the high spots of the moulded design were the low spots of the mould, and vice versa. In industry, similar moulds were used for rubber, plaster, Celluloid (somewhat similar to modern plastics), and other materials. Such designs were achieved by intaglio carving, which requires the carver to think—and carve—in reverse. It is particularly valuable as training for carving smooth hollows or concavities with gouges; a knife is almost useless as a tool for such work. A power rotary tool can be used, but it tends to leave a rough surface onto which the moulded material will stick, as well as to create unintentional undercuts and make what should be straight lines irregular.

Older cookie and butter moulds had simple geometric patterns, and were usually flat boards which were pressed against the material to be moulded;

Fig. 25. A German Springerle roller.

Fig. 26. Springerle cookie-roller patterns.

but as time went on, all sorts of elaborate designs were produced, including coats of arms, initials, and even scenes. For cookie dough, in particular, designs were ultimately carved into a roller similar to a rolling pin, which made the impression more uniform. These rollers decorate *springerle*, a lightly spiced German Christmas cookie.

Designs are carved, largely in single cuts, with small, deep gouges, and detailed with the veiner (itself a very small, deep gouge) and V-tool. Short-bent gouges are helpful but not essential for spherical cuts. Best of all, designs really don't have to be too precise, so you can learn to swing the tool and cut from various angles to accommodate grain. Also, the designs can be put on a flat board rather than on a roller, or used individually for decorative panels.

Preferred woods are light-colored ones with dense grain, like maple or birch. Pine can be used, but the grain tends to rise if the piece gets damp (important only if you plan to make cookies or moulded butter pats). Tools must be very sharp to avoid tearing at cut edges, and sanding should be avoided. If the panels are purely decorative, any wood can be used as long as it isn't too inclined to split. The carving in such a panel can be made more prominent and decorative by "antiquing" with a slightly darker stain. If you plan to do this, first apply a thin coat of matte or satin varnish so the stain doesn't penetrate cross-grain areas unduly and cause undesirable dark areas. If the surface is sealed, stain can be applied and wiped off the surface before it dries, so shading of the color is possible.

Much more elaborate designs can be carved this way. You've undoubtedly seen some, such as the "gingerbread men" from Williamsburg, Virginia. Incised lettering, trade-marks, logotypes, even inverted portraits, such as those carved in shell in Italy, are also possible. (For shell, a rotary tool with grinding wheels does the heavy work.) Note, incidentally, that ridges are difficult because of the problems of smoothing the surfaces around them. The small lines suggesting feathers on a bird or veins in a leaf are all incised (cut in). This makes leaf veins stand out in a cookie as they do in real life, but the feather divisions will stand out rather than being depressed. Optically, this is not unpleasant, and therefore nothing to worry about; but if you do tend to worry, such elements as feathers can, of course, be formed by a series of small cuts with a somewhat flatter gouge. It doesn't affect the taste of the cookie.

CHAPTER VI

Variety in Floral Panels

Foliage can fit the space, shape, use—even the wood

FLOWERS AND FOLIAGE ARE A TRADITIONAL PART of, or decoration on, many other works: plaques, coats of arms, doors, frames, nameplates, boxes, bowls, vases, even handles, chairs and seats. They have been carved as decorations on robes, dresses and hats of 3D figures. All this is undoubtedly because foliage is so adaptable to space requirements and can be made into a non-obtrusive background. It can also convey a concept, such as the oak leaf or acorn for strength, wheat or corn for life, the lily or rose for many religious concepts. Flowers and foliage also have been stylized, as in the Tudor or Luther rose, the acanthus, and the papyrus. Vines have been combined with other motifs to produce openwork screens for all sorts of purposes.

Because they tend to be fragile when carved, flowers and foliage are usually carved in relief rather than in the round. In recent years, much of it has been done in low relief to avoid problems of undercutting and fragility, because foliage is often an integral part of the decoration of utilitarian objects. It is particularly adaptable to filling and closing a circle or other geometric shape, without elaborate and mathematical pre-layout. Thus a design can be carved on the circumference of a bowl, plate, and gourd, with no worry about whether or not the design will "meet itself coming back;" an extra leaf or twist in a stem or vine will compensate. Further, the usual design can itself be expanded or contracted slightly as you go by making flowers a bit wider or narrower, adding leaves and the like. A geometric or other exact pattern will be difficult to accommodate to the changing curvatures of a bowl or vase, but a floral design can simply be pulled in or expanded a little to compensate for changing contours. In fact, the possibilities and variations are so great that I shall try to cover the ground by illustrated examples rather than verbal description.

Figs. 27. (left) Two artificial roses on a store-bought birthday cake inspired me to copy them on a panel (Fig. 28 below). It is, appropriately, of rosewood, about 1 × 6 × 12 in (2.5 × 15 × 30 cm). Elements were drawn on it, then the background was routed ½ in (12.7 mm) deep and the units were modelled. Background was scalloped with a flat gouge.

Fig. 29. More than 40 years ago, Gardner Wood carved some original designs on furniture for me. This floral swag is on the back of a mahogany dining-room chair.

Fig. 30. This hanging shelf was made by a self-taught Indian carver in Pátzcuaro, Mexico. It is of pine, and the flowing floral patterns were created by "chip carving"—cutting crescents with a gouge.

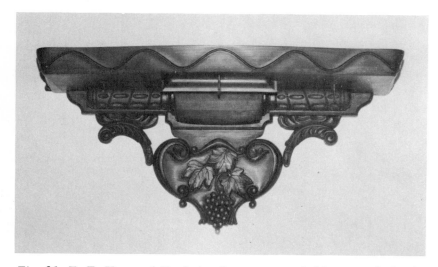

Fig. 31. T. E. Haag, of Tualatin, Oregon, carved this grape design into a cherry-wood shelf.

Figs. 32–33–34. The dogwood pattern (bottom) used on this salad bowl (top) and the napkin rings (center) was copied from the actual flower and leaf of the dogwood. The pieces are in myrtle, which has strong color variations. The bowl was finished with a gloss varnish outside, vegetable oil inside; the rings were gloss-varnished.

DOGWOOD MOTIF on a salad bowl

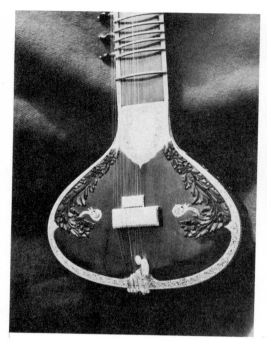

Figs. 35–36–37. Some of the best decorative floral carving is done on sitars in India. This one is especially elaborate, with inlays on the face (left) and carving on back (above) and resonator (below), made from a gourd.

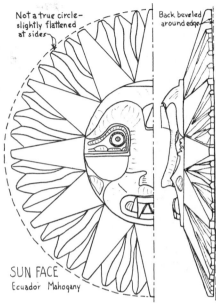

SUN FACE
Ecuador Mahogany

Figs. 38–39. (above and right) This mahogany sun caricature is 4½ in (11 cm) across the face, 9½ in (24 cm) across the rays, and was carved in Ecuador.

Fig. 40. (below) Decorative plaques often incorporate foliage (as do coats of arms). This walnut plate was made by Gunther Goetz, of Denton, Texas.

CHAPTER VII

Entrancing Entrances

Doors take to foliage and fancy—and vice versa

DOORS HAVE ALWAYS BEEN SYMBOLIC as well as functional: they bar the world or invite it to enter, but in either case they are the focus of the building and, as a result, have received special attention from architects, builders, and owners. Carved doors, usually highly individualized, are familiar, particularly on public buildings—their flat surfaces invite decoration.

Both foliage and fanciful beasts have been common motifs in design, alone or mixed with geometric patterns, scenic panels, busts or other significant elements for highlights. The doors pictured here are only a sampling of what can be done, but they range from the blocky carving of stylized animals in Fiji (Fig. 41) through a very appropriate grape pattern in Peru (Fig. 42), and a traditional foliage scroll in Spain (Fig. 44), to the many variations possible in Moorish distortion of the Arab alphabet to obtain a scroll pattern of a holy phrase (Fig. 45).

Fig. 41.

Figs. 42–43. The double doors of a winery in Pisco, Peru, are also an advertisement for its product. They show the juice of the grape entering the characteristically shaped aging jars.

Figs. 44–45. The two examples (on this and the facing page) of Mudejar (Moorish) carving are from doors in the 14th-century Taller del Moro (Shop of the Moor) in Toledo, Spain. Here, traditional leaf patterns are combined with Arabic letters.

CHAPTER VIII

Floral Polyglot Panels

SOME YEARS AGO, I CARVED a number of polyglot panels in teak, grouping animals in one, birds in another, "bugs" in still another, and so on. These all evolved from my so-called "bug tree," which was a polyglot group of insects, worms and spiders carved in heroic size on the 12-ft (3.6-m) trunk of an apple tree they had conspired to kill. Units were placed where they fitted and as whim dictated, without regard to relative scale or viewing aspect. This *stele*, or column, was in reality a carved panel wrapped around a tree.

This panel (Fig. 46) is a lineal descendant—a commission for one panel featuring flowers and birds. I had available a plank 12 in (30 cm) wide, of English sycamore (harewood) which is very white and dense, with a crossfire figure in fiddle pattern, enough to give the wood interest without being obtrusive. It is amenable to both chisel and knife, does not split or crumble, and will support a great deal of detail. (It is customarily a veneer, used as an alternate to American holly, and as the client was English, the wood was a happy choice.)

Panel width was about 10½ in (26 cm), so I selected a length of 17½ in (44 cm—the "Golden Mean" calls for a width 60 percent of height), which, with a reasonable self-border all around, left a 9 × 16-in (23 × 40-cm) working area. The panel thickness was 1 in (2.5 cm). I decided on a background depth of only ⅛ in (3.2 mm), with limited modelling of elements. Birds and flowers drawn from field guides were laid out directly on the wood. I tried to select birds and flowers that are familiar and have distinctive silhouettes, and I altered scale to make the subject fit the space. Layout and carving were done simultaneously from one corner. Slight overlaps are advisable to avoid gaps and the stringy look of straight stems, of course, and care must be taken not to "carve oneself into a corner." As my panel worked out, it included 62 birds and five flowers.

Because the carving was relatively shallow and the wood so white, I darkened the background with a light-tan, German, sal-ammoniac stain to make the elements stand out. This was preceded by a spray coat of matte varnish to avoid over-absorption of stain in cross-grain areas. The carved surface was also coated with the same stain, but in small areas at a time, so the stain could be wiped off again at once, leaving high spots almost white, with darker lines.

You probably won't want to make an exactly similar panel. The designs are flexible, so you can make another arrangement or use them individually. I have included a sketch and index for identification of design elements I used on a walrus tusk of the same design (Fig. 47). Like the bug tree, it is

Fig. 46. Polyglot panel of English syca-more depicts 62 birds and five flowers selected for familiarity and distinctive silhouette (see Fig. 48).

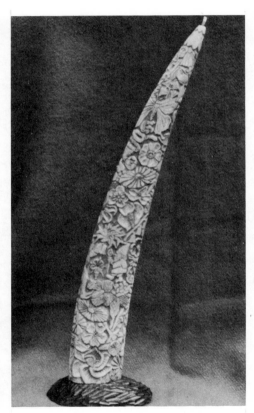

Fig. 47. A polyglot panel of 94 flowers, four birds, four insects, a gnome and a worm was "wrapped around" an 18-in (46-cm) walrus tusk (see Fig. 49).

43

Fig. 48. Polyglot panel of English sycamore is 1 × 10½ × 17½ in (2.5 × 27 × 44 cm).

Identification: Flower and Bird Panel (Illus. 48)

Flowers

1. Blue vervain
2. Wild sunflower
3. Columbine, or 4-o'clock
4. Frangipani
5. Queen Anne's lace
6. Jack-in-the-Pulpit
7. Oxeye Daisy
8. Heliconia
9. Purple coneflower
10. Common plantain
11. Trumpet creeper
12. Shooting star, or American cowslip
13. Jewelweed
14. Morning glory
15. Tulip
16. Day lily
17. Purple virgin's-bower (clematis)
18. Evening primrose
19. Dandelion
20. Dayflower
21. Lousewort
22. Oswego tea, or bee balm
23. American lotus (a water lily)
24. Black-eyed susan
25. Angel's-trumpet (small tree)
26. Lily-of-the-valley
27. Wood anemone
28. Atamasco lily
29. Iris
30. Painted trillium
31. Flowering dogwood
32. Skunk cabbage
33. Clover
34. Wild rose
35. Lady-slipper (yellow)
36. Forget-me-not
37. Thistle
38. Nightshade
39. Water arum
40. Bluebell
41. Fringed gentian
42. Bottle gentian
43. Buttercup
44. Rose mallow
45. Anthurium
46. Coral trumpet (floweret)
47. White violet
48. Bluet or innocence
49. Bird-of-paradise
50. Marsh marigold
51. Pitcher plant
52. Hibiscus
53. Daffodil
54. Indian pipe
55. Plantain (water reed)
56. Water lily
57. Indian pink
58. Wild ginger
59. Cow or yellow pond-lily
60. Wild geranium
61. Cattail
62. Moss pink

Birds

A. Ruby-throated humming-bird
B. House wren
C. Cardinal
D. Robin
E. Saw-whet owl

Key to Patterns—Walrus-Tusk Floral Stele

1. Solitary gentian
2. Columbine, or 4-o'clock
3. Jack-in-the-pulpit
4. Purple coneflower
5. Bluet, or innocence
6. Jewelweed
7. Coral trumpet (floweret)
8. Yellow lady-slipper
9. Evening primrose
10. Blue vervain
11. Bottle gentian
12. Sundrops
13. Dayflower
14. Ten-petalled sunflower
15. Ruby-throated hummingbird
16. Purple virgin's-bower (a clematis)
17. Tiger swallowtail (butterfly)
18. Shooting star, or American cowslip
19. Heliconia
20. Dutchman's-pipe
21. Skunk cabbage
22. Tulip
23. Hedge bindweed, or wild morning glory
24. American lotus (a water lily)
25. Swamp rose
26. Brantling (spatulate-tailed earthworm)
27. Queen Anne's lace, or cow lily
28. Cowslip
29. Large-flowered trillium
30. Wintergreen
31. Nightshade, or bittersweet
32. Indian paint-brush, or painted cup
33. House wren
34. Bull thistle
35. Dutchman's-breeches
36. Black-eyed susan
37. Indian pink
38. Star-of-Bethlehem
39. Turtlehead
40. Atamasco lily
41. American rhododendron
42. Mountain laurel
43. Yellow clover
44. Day lily
45. American cardinal
46. Forget-me-not
47. Anthurium
48. Lily-of-the-valley
49. Rose mallow
50. Lousewort, or wood betony
51. Oswego tea, or bee balm
52. Flowering dogwood
53. Iris
54. Buttercup
55. Daffodil
56. Violet
57. Indian pipe
58. Solomon's seal
59. Gnome
60. Water arum
61. Robber fly
62. Corn cockle
63. Pitcher plant
64. Sundew
65. Monkshood, or aconite
66. Frangipani
67. Fringed gentian
68. Angel's-trumpet
69. Ladybug
70. Amaryllis
71. Bird-of-paradise flower

72. Hibiscus
73. Cactus flower
74. Red ginger
75. Dragonfly
76. Wood anemone
77. Whorled pogonia
78. Indian pink, or arethusa
79. Saxifrage
80. Milkweed
81. Monarch butterfly
82. Monkey flower
83. Cattail
84. Shrimp plant
85. Oxeye daisy
86. Maiden pink
87. Ragged robin
88. Dandelion
89. Chickweed
90. Water lily
91. Common speedwell
92. Bellwort
93. Arrowhead
94. Saw-whet owl
95. Moss pink
96. Jasmine
97. Bromeliad (air plant)
98. Oleander
99. Tree hibiscus
100. Honolulu rose
101. Wild ginger
102. New England aster
103. Mayapple
104. Golden club

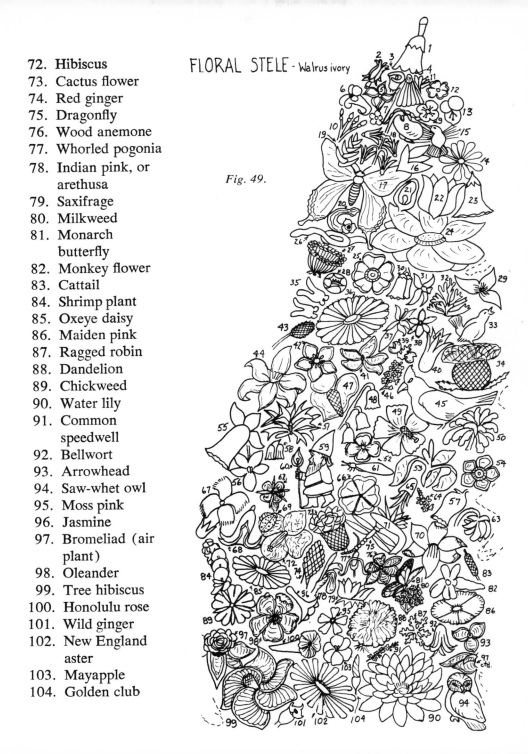

FLORAL STELE - Walrus ivory

Fig. 49.

essentially a panel wrapped around a pillar, allowing for variations in pillar shape and size. Because this is ivory and very supportive of detail, I could make the elements smaller, thus accommodating more. On a tusk 18 in (45 cm) long and about 2 × 3 in (5 × 7.5 cm) at its oval base, I worked in 94 flowers, four birds, four insects, a gnome, and a worm—or 104 subjects in all. Ivory can be carved with conventional tools: veiner, V-tool, fluter, small gouges and firmers. It is advisable to put the material on a cushioned surface and to use a light mallet.

Details are carved with a knife, many of them with a concave blade in a chuck handle. Such a blade is thick enough to stand the load. It's like carving ebony or lignum vitae: many small cuts, more patience, and frequent tool dressing. I drilled the tip of the tusk to insert a stem in the solitary gentian there. Ivory, like the harewood, is very white, so detail cannot be seen without help under most lighting. The Chinese take care of that problem by staining with strong tea, or with candle or incense smoke, wiped off the high spots. Such materials do not penetrate the surface of ivory to any extent, and cross-grain can be neglected, so surface preparation isn't necessary. I simply used the same light-tan stain, and thoroughly wiped it off the surface. The result is a stele appraised at over 1,000 dollars (425 pounds).

CHAPTER IX

Portrait of a Pine

How to simplify foliage and retain identity

TREES, CLOUDS AND SPLASHING WATER can be the nemesis of a woodcarver because all have feathery, ill-defined edges, and a carving tends to make them look rigid and blocky. Therefore, it was with some trepidation that I undertook this panel portrait of a particular pine tree (Fig. 50). It was planted almost 40 years ago by the client's son, and both have since grown taller and older, although the pine had suffered from the breaking of an upper fork that had stripped branches down one side; hence it was somewhat misshapen. The finished panel was to be accompanied by some very special verses written by the client about the tree and the growing child, so it had to be personal and whimsical in feeling.

Obviously, it was impractical to depict every needle, or even every little branch. As in making a portrait of a person, it was advisable to idealize, *not* caricature, the subject a little. Thus it was helpful to fill out a few scrawny branches and to remove interferences around the tree or in the background, as well as to picture it from the side that is usually seen. It was also essential to retain the identifiable shape of the trunk and larger branches as well as major elements of the surrounding terrain. Yet one can justifiably add a little animal life or slightly move a bush or the like in the interest of a better composition—that's "artistic license."

I began by taking a series of photographs of the tree to get the overall shape and the effect of perspective on the eye of the viewer from the usual viewing point as well as from others. These turned out to be less helpful than I had anticipated, because a picture taken against the sky—even on a snowy and relatively dark day—loses considerable detail because of the contrast. I could, however, determine general shape and composition and lay the tree out on a 2 × 12 × 19-in (5 × 30 × 47.5-cm) Oregon-pine panel, then go to the site and sketch in added detail. I made no preliminary sketch because there was no need for that kind of a record or guide, and I used pine because it was relatively soft and because it was the same material as the subject. The step-by-step pictures tell the rest of the story (Figs. 51 to 55).

Portrait of a pine, step by step

(**Fig. 50**) Of the seven pictures taken, this one was most helpful to attain general shape, including the masses of needles and the slight curve of the trunk as well as the disfigurement where the fork had broken years ago. However, the needle masses obscured the actual branch positions. The brush around the tree base and a neighbor's shed beyond the fence, as well as the trees in the background, were left out of the final composition as primarily confusing factors, although the fence and an adjacent bush and small hemlock were included.

Fig. 50.

(**Fig. 51**) The tree was drawn directly on the block by the point-to-point method. Fortunately, the carving was to be exactly three times the size of the key photo, so transfer of dimensions was relatively easy, although detailed.

Fig. 51.

Fig. 52.

Some branches could be placed by eye, others modified slightly in the interest of better composition. It is also important to remember that extremely small openings between branches and elsewhere should be avoided when possible because of the difficulty in carving them. The fence is cross-grain and difficult, but unavoidable. The sketch was modified by direct observation of the tree, then blocking outlines were inked in.

(**Fig. 52**) Setting-in and grounding-out are extremely tedious and painstaking in this case, but essential to retain the character of the tree. Setting-in must be done carefully to avoid breaking of narrow cross-grain sections. One way to reduce this likelihood is to set-in the second side of a narrow section by driving in the chisel at an angle *away* from the opposite side, then later correcting the cut to vertical. Also, depth must be severely limited in such cuts, at least initially. (As you get deeper, the danger of breakout is reduced.)

51

I selected a ground depth of ½ in (12.7 mm) as most practical. For setting in, I lined in with a veiner, and set-in with a ¼-in (6.3-mm) firmer, ⅟₁₆-in (1.6-mm) flat gouge (#3), ¼-in (6.3-mm) medium gouge (#5), plus knife and hook knife. Grounding required the same tools, plus a ⅜-in (9.6-mm) deep gouge (#7).

(**Fig. 53**) Grounding could be left quite rough and cleaned up as modelling proceeded. To suggest the needle structure, I used parallel cuts with the veiner, or vees with the knife, depending upon the size of the area. Each branch was first modelled to a general shape, and the branch itself suggested by cutting a vee on each side of it, usually with the knife to avoid breakouts. A V-tool might have been used, but it would have caused trouble because of narrow sections and cross-grain cuts. Even the veiner caused some trouble, although it was razor-sharp. As carving progressed, I modified the original sketch here and there to suggest branches on the face that had been stripped.

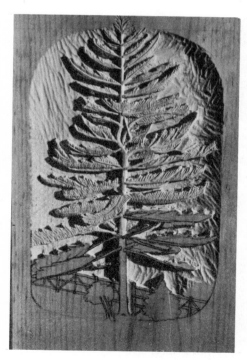

Fig. 53.

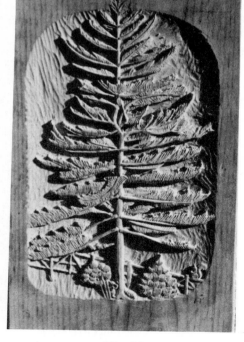

Fig. 54.

Also note that the branches are quite visible at the top of the tree but are obscured lower down because of the point of view of an observer. Needles are not continuous lines in one direction; they vary across a branch to suggest multiplicity. The lines are also carried down the set-in sides to the ground, to break the solid look of the edge as much as possible.

(**Fig. 54**) A bird to scale on a tree of this size would be almost invisible, and a bird flying in the sky would be both a nuisance and somewhat trite, so I carved a slightly oversized bird alighting on an upper left-hand branch. As carving progressed, I also added a squirrel sitting on the fence and a raccoon peering around the base, although the raccoon is essentially a night animal, at least in my suburban area.

As carving was completed, it was necessary to reduce the prominence of some branches and leaf structures, and to emphasize others, as well as to clean up the ground after set-in sides were textured. I also elected to leave tool marks on the background in a somewhat haphazard pattern, although they were principally vertical to reduce tearing of edges. These were cut with the deep gouge as far as possible. Light sanding was done in some areas, particularly on branches and on rough portions of the background. Then the entire panel was given two coats of spray matte varnish, "antiqued" with teak stain, and waxed.

Fig. 55.

CHAPTER X

Carve the Little Mermaid

CERTAINLY ONE OF THE BEST-KNOWN NUDES in the world is the Little Mermaid who sits forlornly on a boulder in the harbor of Copenhagen, Denmark. I had seen a great many pictures of her, but when I decided to carve a miniature, all I could find immediately was a color photo I had taken years before. I projected that to a 6-in (15-cm) height and copied it for my basic pattern, deciding to develop the figure as I carved. I guessed that a 6-in (15-cm) figure would be a bit under 4 in (10 cm) through, even posed at the angle of my available photograph, and I had a piece of mahogany 4 × 10 × 10 in (10 × 25 × 25 cm), slightly checked on the top, and therefore discarded by a nearby piano maker. By the time I had the figure roughed out, I had also found an additional photograph (Fig. 56) through the Danish Information Service in New York. They helped but were frontal views, so the Mermaid's back had to be largely improvised.

The procedure outlined by the step-by-step photographs (Figs. 57 to 71) can, however, be applied to any copy from a photograph or painting, and most will be far less exacting. As you will note, my version is a bit more plump and buxom than Edvard Eriksen's original, and makes her look a little older. The original mermaid, according to the story by Hans Christian Andersen, was a 16-year-old who fell in love at first sight with an earthly prince when she made her first trip to the surface of the sea. She saved his life in a shipwreck, but had to leave him on shore, where another girl found him and revived him. Although the mermaid sacrificed her tongue, her 300-year life, and her tail to become an earthling, the prince eventually married the other girl, and the mermaid became a mere spirit of the air.

The story I read has her changing directly from tail to legs and feet, but the sculptor shows her with attenuated feet and fins up and down shin and calf, so I made her the same way. You may recall, also, that some years back vandals beheaded her. The Danish government found the original plaster model and replaced the head, complete with downcast mouth and sad eyes—but no tears. Mermaids cannot cry.

Fig. 56. The Little Mermaid, made by Danish sculptor Edvard Eriksen, is the symbolic statue of Copenhagen. She sits on her stone at the entrance to Copenhagen Harbor. (Photo copyright Royal Danish Ministry for Foreign Affairs.)

The Mermaid step-by-step

(**Fig. 58**) Lay out the silhouette on a planed side, using a template or carbon paper, and reinforce the lines with a soft-tip pen. If possible, lay out the back as well (if you can be sure to make it match exactly in position). If you have a bandsaw, you can now saw out the shape. I used a carpenter's crosscut saw and ripsaw, sawing straight lines to salvage the wood at upper corners. A coping saw can be used, but it is extremely slow and somewhat inaccurate on a 4-in (10-cm) thickness. Shorter cuts can be made about the head, then the profile is roughed to shape with a 1-in (25-mm) flat gouge or equivalent. Roughing should be about ⅛ in (3.2 mm) outside guidelines at crucial points. The parallel-faced base can be clamped in a vise for this.

(**Fig. 59**) A double template will prove helpful in the next few steps. The interior template or pattern will provide the base line of the figure itself and makes early checking easy. The outer template is of little use until final-shaping of the silhouette. Plastic, cardboard, or paper can be used; I used notepaper in this instance because these templates have short-term functions.

(**Fig. 60**) Bring the silhouette fairly accurately to shape. The safe way to do this is to draw lines across with a square at critical points, and to then cut guidelines with a deep ¼-in (6.3-mm) gouge or a fluter. Check these guide-lines with the square to be sure that they are square with the outer faces and of uniform depth across the block; they generally tend to be high in the middle. (I have left one or two gouge lines to show what I mean.) Now, with the 1-in (25.4-mm) gouge, fair the surfaces to just outside the guidelines, using the channels and the square to check for accuracy. *Do not* detail the face or fingertip silhouettes; leave wood there in case you need it later. Be as accurate as you can because the next steps will destroy your outline of the figure as well as much of the flat faces, which are reference surfaces.

(**Fig. 61**) The side view (if one is available) could now be copied on the blank and the side silhouette sawed out. But I had only a front view and didn't trust my side sketches implicitly, particularly because the mermaid is at an angle to the faces of the boulder (as was my original photo and the silhouette). Therefore, I started with her left leg almost parallel to the boulder front face, and cut back the front of the block at an angle which would place her toe ¼ in (6 mm) in from the block edge, and her left knee about ¾ in (19 mm)

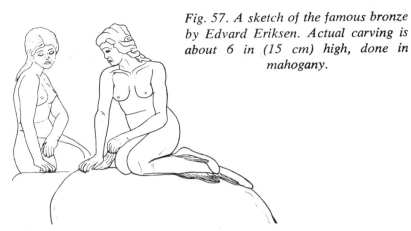

Fig. 57. A sketch of the famous bronze by Edvard Eriksen. Actual carving is about 6 in (15 cm) high, done in mahogany.

Fig. 58.

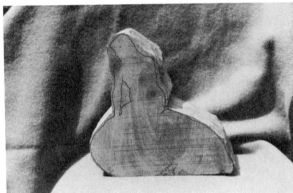

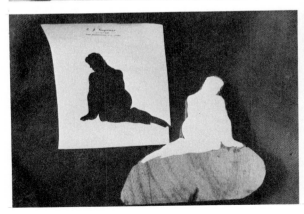

Fig. 59.

Fig. 60.

(**Fig. 62**) Lay out the knee positions and cut back the face of the block to expose the right knee. You will need V-tool, ¼-in (6-mm) and ⅛-in (3-mm) firmers; the 1-in (2.5-cm) gouge is too big. Now begin to form the legs, shaping the lower legs and allowing wood for the fins. (Unlike the usual mermaid, she does not have a tail; instead, her feet are over-long and she has fins extending from the shinbone, back of the calf, and the heel.) Locating and shaping the feet and knees will provide the approximate location of the buttocks, and shaping the leg gives the point of contact of left elbow and thigh. When this is approximated, the arm can be laid out and roughed. Corners of the boulder have been rounded in front merely for convenience and comfort in handling.

(**Fig. 63**) Set in the outline of the left arm and cut away wood above and below, sloping the shoulder back at the same time. Remember not to cut out wood high on the chest; you must leave wood for the left breast, which projects forward of the arm. Also, the right knee is in back of the left, and the line of the knee fronts will establish the line of the shoulders and buttocks fairly accurately, because her torso is not twisted. To locate a given point on the blank, place the template accurately over such surface as you can, and stick a straight pin through the desired spot into the wood. In cutting the arm, leave a little extra wood where possible for shaping. It is easy to cut away wood, but difficult to put it back.

(**Fig. 64**) Establish the lines of the breast bottoms and the cutout between right arm and body. Shape the breasts and cut away between them and the left arm. Also bring the right shoulder back so that it is behind the left one, a little less than parallel to the knee fronts. Begin the cutout between right arm and body. This must be done very carefully, or you'll be short of wood for the right or left arm.

(**Fig. 65**) Begin to cut the stomach well back, particularly on the right side. The mermaid is not sitting erect, but is slumped over in grief, which accounts for the slightly forward hunch of the shoulders and the exceptional hollowing of the stomach. It will also account later for a rounding of the middle of the back. It may be of assistance at this point to rough out the shape of the hollow between right arm and body and to begin to define the face as a reference. Note that I have merely indicated the nose, which makes quick relocation of the template possible. Once the line of the nose is established (front to back), the back of the head can be cut away to the shoulder in preparation for locating the neck. Also cut away wood above the breasts and prepare to locate the right hand by cutting back at the wrist. In this pose, the mermaid is not resting on her right hand—the heel of the hand is actually slightly raised so that her weight is essentially on her right buttock (which will be lower than the left because she is sitting on her feet, which extend to the left).

(**Fig. 66**) By sighting from the side, locate the rough line of the back and begin to remove wood there. Don't go too far initially: remember that the curved back and the weight on the right buttock will cause it to bulge slightly. However, the buttocks should be in line with the knees. Also, if you haven't done so previously, shape the legs and feet, allowing for the fins, and round off the boulder behind them to the general shape. Don't chamfer it yet, because we are still in doubt about the precise position of the right buttock. The same goes for the back of the head, because that depends upon where the front of the head ultimately will be. Also, begin to shape the left arm and to hole through just above the elbow, which will establish the line (depth in from the front) of that side of the stomach.

(**Fig. 67**) Now it is time to establish the lines of the back and the right arm. Begin by creating the hollow on the left side behind the elbow, then round the back, remembering that her back is a curve from top to bottom because her pose is one of utter dejection. Also, work in from the right side around and behind the hand so that you can establish that buttocks line. Lay out the rough banjo-shape of the back, and round the buttocks and waist to agree with the left side. I found at this point that I had estimated the top of the back of the rock almost ¼ in (6 mm) too high, because the right buttock was obviously too shallow and was not enough below the left to make the pose natural. When the top was lowered, the left foot gained needed thickness as well.

(**Fig. 68**) With the general shape of the back worked out, draw in the line of the spine. Basically, it is a curve from the base to the waist, then bends to rise almost straight up. Also round the back of the right shoulder and continue to shape the back and right buttock, working carefully on the latter so that it is in line (with respect to both height and position) with the right knee. It will help, at this point, to remove the wood behind the left arm, down to the level of the thigh. The right thigh, by the way, is almost horizontal on top, front to back, rather than rising as the left one does. It is also sensible, at this point, to hollow out between the thighs under the left arm, a tricky job that requires small tools like fluter, veiner, and a small firmer or flat gouge,

Fig. 61.

Fig. 62.

Fig. 63.

Fig. 64.

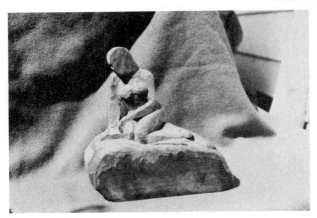

Fig. 65.

preferably $\frac{1}{16}$ in (1.6 mm), or a long-tipped knife blade. The left wrist is actually free of the right thigh, but I would not cut it loose yet.

(**Fig. 69**) Now shape the right arm, particularly at the shoulder, to establish the line of the upper chest and breasts. This will, in turn, provide the base of the neck and the general location of the head, which is turned to the right so that the line of the nose is about midway between right nipple and right shoulder. You can also begin to rough out the head, rounding it on top and

Fig. 66.

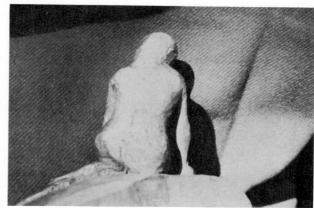

Fig. 67.

establishing the general hairline, so the face can be positioned below it. You will probably find, as I did, that the upper back should be thinned and rounded more, and that the breasts are too large and too far forward. Also, there must be a crease across the stomach because of her stooped position.

(**Fig. 70**) Shape the cloth below her left hand and the hand itself. The hand should hang, half closed, from the wrist, with the cloth caught between thumb and first finger and trailing from the fingertips. Cut a deep vee beneath the wrist to lift the hand from the right knee. (This can be sawed through with

Fig. 68.

Fig. 69.

a thin blade, but will be stronger if left solid in back.) Shape the face, chin, and neck and carve the face, remembering that her mouth should curve down at the corners to show dejection. Be sure the line of the right shoulder is low enough as it joins the hairline so a bit of the neck shows on the right. You will probably have to thin the neck. I did all of this work with knives, one of which had a concave edge.

(**Fig. 71**) Finish the right hand and lift it from the rock by undercutting. The heel of the hand should be up almost ¼ in (6 mm) so the fingertips can turn down and in. To reduce the blocky effect of the base, round the front corners, put in a notch on the front, and lower the right rear top of the rock. To get a coarse, open texture such as a rock would have, I sanded it with a

Fig. 70.

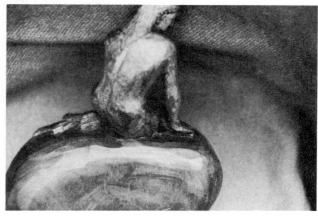

Fig. 71.

rotary sander to fair-in knife cuts at the same time, then finished with fairly coarse paper near the figure. The figure itself is not sanded, so that the small planes left by the knife will catch the light. This also increases the contrast between girl and rock.

A final word: Once the figure is finished, set it aside for a day, then look at it again, *closely*. You will find a number of fine changes to make. I spent two hours, for example, thinning down and shaping the right arm and shoulder, another two hours removing fine burrs and other imperfections elsewhere.

The figure was finished with spray matte (satin) varnish and clear shoe polish. I made a number of changes thereafter, and found that I could mask them completely by rubbing in a bit of polyester varnish in the shaved spots, wiping it off, then applying new coats of shoe polish over the area.

Fig. 72. The completed carving, finished in wax. Tool marks were left to emphasize the fact that she is wood, and the boulder base has been reduced in thickness to suit the wood available.

CHAPTER XI

Carving Can Be Heroic

Bigger than life, these sculptures can be group efforts

THE "TREE OF LIFE," CARVED BY LAURENCE TENNEY STEVENS from a 60-ft (18-m) length of 155-year-old elm for the 1939 New York World's Fair, was probably the tallest one-piece heroic sculpture ever produced on this continent. There are one or two Western totem poles that are taller, but they are not single subjects, nor do they have integral limbs.

A number of heroic figures have, however, been carved in recent years in various parts of the United States, including several of Indians, one of Paul Bunyan, and one of Sir Walter Raleigh. Of these, the tallest is a 62-ft (18.5-m) Skowhegan Indian, carved from native Maine pine by Bernard Langlais of Cushing, Maine, in 1969, Maine's 150th anniversary as a state. It now stands in the town of Skowhegan on a concrete base resembling a series of ledges. It is not a one-piece construction, however. The Indian has a fish weir of interwoven poles in his right hand and a fish spear in his left, in memory of the salmon-fishing in the Penobscot River. The figure is finished in "natural" color, with painted decoration on shoulders, skirt edge and feathers, plus stained face, arms and hair. Mr. Langlais studied sculpture in the United States, France and Norway, and developed a somewhat stylized, straight-line design for this figure.

Also in Maine is a 31-ft (9-m) statue of Paul Bunyan, the legendary lumberjack. The stories have it that Paul weighed 50 lb (22.5 kg) at birth, and soon outgrew houses and had to sleep out-of-doors. Another legend claims that rocking his cradle caused the high tides on Penobscot Bay, and that the Maine lakes are in the footprints of Paul and Babe, the blue ox (as are Minnesota's 10,000 lakes—which Downeasters contend were made on a visit there by Paul). Furthermore, Paul hung up the Northern Lights to get an 18-hour day at his "biggest" lumbering camp and scuffed out the Great

Lakes with his boot to give Babe a drinking hole. His legend is perpetuated by the statue in Bangor, Maine.

A 24-ft (7-m) cypress statue of Sir Walter Raleigh now stands on Roanoke Island, North Carolina. It was carved by R. K. Harniman in 1975 as part of the preparations for the American Bicentennial, and took about ten months to complete. The log itself was contributed by Weyerhaeuser Lumber, and was the third felled in their search for a sound log of proper dimensions. It weighed 12 tons (5 metric tons) and a path had to be bulldozed to it, through the eastern North Carolina swamp where it grew. Other local firms provided hauling, erection and a 2½-ton (2¼-metric-ton) welded-steel base. The log was erected on the base in the atrium of a Raleigh, North Carolina, shopping

Fig. 73. "Tree of Life" at 1939 New York World's Fair was 60 ft (18 m) tall, carved in a 155-year-old Connecticut elm by Laurence Tenney Stevens. It is flanked by two smaller heroic figures.

Fig. 74. Paul Bunyan, at Bangor, Maine, is 31 ft (9 m) tall. Peavey and ax heads are steel; base is built up of native stone. (Maine Department of Commerce and Industry photo.)

Fig. 75. The Skowhegan Indian is a 62-ft (19-m) assembled pine statue in Skowhegan, Maine. Forearms, spear and weir are added elements. (Maine Department of Commerce and Industry photo.)

mall before carving began. It was inverted, so a forked section provided the legs, and sections of the same log were pegged and glued in place for the arms. A flow under the right arm was filled with concrete, then faced with wood as well. Carving was started with a chain saw and finished with mallet and chisels to leave a gouge-textured surface.

Harniman worked from a 3-ft (90-cm) clay model. He chose cypress because it grows large enough for his purposes, its shrinkage from drying is only about 2 percent, and it is not prone to check. It is also extremely durable. The figure now stands exposed to the weather, but is protected by transparent plastic-base coatings. The tree was, by the way, 507 years old when it was felled.

Because his New Haven, Connecticut, studio was vandalized, Harniman now lives in a van, as does Peter Toth, who has been going from state to state carving large busts from local trees as monuments to American Indians. He has carved more than 35, including a 24-ft (7-m) oak figure on display in Charles Towne Landing, South Carolina.

Discarded utility poles, usually cedar, have been the basis of many Boy Scout totem poles. I made one myself about 55 years ago, using a shingling hatchet for much of the roughing. But Bill Butterfield of the Viking Chapter of the National Wood Carvers Association, in Minneapolis-St. Paul, Minnesota, has come up with a different wrinkle: a group of three poles, each with panel designs carved in its face. The poles are inverted so that the thick ends are up, helping the perspective when the 30-ft (9-m) or so, assembly is viewed from the ground. Whether a single pole—as for a Cub Scout camp—or a group, all of his poles have a theme: the American Bicentennial, the history of electricity, and the like.

The group has evolved a practical approach to the problem of carving the poles. Sketches suiting the theme are made by a local artist or developed from library research by the carvers. They are enlarged to suitable size in an overhead projector and the design is transferred to the pole by placing it in position, then going over it with a knurled wheel. The resulting dots are connected by waterproof soft-tipped pen (other markings have a tendency to fade in the sun or wash away in the rain). The pole itself is laid on rail ties and rotated, if necessary, by cant hook.

Roughing can be speeded with a chain saw, even if only for outlining the panels. The background is about 2 in (5 cm) deep and can be knocked out readily with large chisels. Woodcarving tools are used only for the detail, which can be surprisingly fine: even portraits have been carved recognizably.

There is sufficient demand from local governments, parks, Scout and other camps, shopping malls, and even libraries to use the product, and the donee will usually arrange for a flatbed trailer or truck to carry the poles to and from the carving area, while the local utility will provide erecting equipment. Best of all, it is a group project—as many as 20 carvers have worked on one pole—and can be done where the public can watch.

Webster defines "heroic" as "larger than life-size, but smaller than colossal." On this basis, the carved utility poles are not heroic sculpture, because the individual designs are only life-size or smaller. Neither are the others that I

Fig. 76. Sir Walter Raleigh is in cypress and stands 24 ft (7 m) tall, including the 5-ft (2-m) welded-steel base. Arms are pegged and glued in place, and entire figure is coated with transparent plastic-base coatings. It is now on Roanoke Island, North Carolina. (Photo by J. Foster Scott, Dare City Tourist Bureau.)

Neqro
Thai

Top left to bottom left:
Figs. 77–78. Three old cedar utility poles are combined in this tall sculpture, with separate cap. It stands about 30 ft (9 m) high, in front of a Minneapolis utility building. Details of design shown in close-up sketch (Fig. 78). Fig. 79. Steel bands bind together the three cedar poles that form this sculpture in a Minneapolis park. Like the other obelisk in Fig. 77, it was carved by as many as 20 members of the Viking Chapter National Woodcarvers Association. (Photos of the poles taken by J. Douglas Carver, Plymouth, Minnesota.) Fig. 80. Temple guardians in Thailand are heroic figures, usually of teak. This is a copy of the guardian monkey head, made as a mask.

have shown, although Ed Jaffe's Indian head is upwards of 15 in (28 cm) tall. The Madonna from Easter Island approaches heroic size, however, and was the cooperative work of a group of carvers, as were the utility poles. Its design is such that it could have been made larger—and would have been except that Easter Island has no bigger trees. The temple-guardian masks are copied directly from much larger heroic figures which stand at temple doorways in various parts of Thailand. They are usually polychromed and gilded. In Japan, temple guardians may be demons, monkeys, lions, or whatever, and similar heroic figures stand outside temples throughout the Orient. It is there, also, that truly colossal statues of the Buddha have been made, some carved of assembled wood, then cased in gold or other materials. The point is, I suppose, that all over the world, man strives to produce something bigger than himself, something bigger than life.

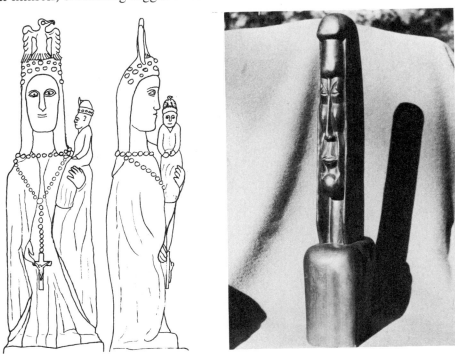

Fig. 81. Our Lady of Rapa Nui was another group effort, done by twelve Easter Island carvers in 1970. The design lends itself to one-piece production. Fig. 82. Attenuated Indian head was Ed Jaffe's first go at woodcarving. It is in mahogany, on a 6-in (15-cm) base.

CHAPTER XII

Thor and His Hammer

THOR, THE THUNDERER, WAS THE NORDIC GOD of physical prowess and thunderstorms. He wielded a hammer called Mjöllnir which returned to his glove after accomplishing its mission. The thrown hammer caused thunder, so it had its own personality, like the weapons of other mythic figures. Such a hammer must obviously have a special shape; therefore, I've chosen the one that I think would wield and fly best.

Depictions of Thor range from youthful and lithe to ancient and long-bearded, and from nude to heavily cloaked. I drew him in the first fashion but carved him somewhat more mature. He is a rather straightforward figure

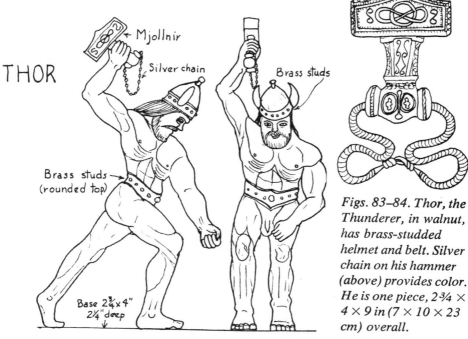

THOR

Mjollnir

Silver chain

Brass studs

Brass studs
(rounded top)

Base 2¾ x 4"
2¼" deep

Figs. 83–84. Thor, the Thunderer, in walnut, has brass-studded helmet and belt. Silver chain on his hammer (above) provides color. He is one piece, 2¾ × 4 × 9 in (7 × 10 × 23 cm) overall.

offering no real problems. I posed him in action, so musculature was important, but be careful not to make him so heavily muscled that he becomes grotesque. I designed .him to fit an available piece of walnut, but avoided stiffness by thrusting his elbows out to the limit of the wood thickness and pulling in his shoulders and hips. (Shoulders that are the full thickness of the available wood necessitate arms that hang straight down or go straight up, so the figure tends to look stiff and unnatural.) I carved him complete with base.

Once the side outline is roughed in, the wood can be thinned around the head and extended arm so that a scrollsaw can be used efficiently to approach the exact outline. As always, however, maintain the drawn centerline on the blank, replacing it in each area as that area is shaped, and replace the body outlines on the side. Also, do all the heavy carving of the upper portions before the legs are separated, so there is plenty of strength at the base. Because the figure is carved complete with base, it can be clamped in a conventional vise for sawing and rough cutting, yet is small enough to be held in the hand for whittling of details.

Thor's pose is unusual in that the right leg, rather than the left, is forward. I felt that this was correct, considering that Thor is throwing downward from an eminence rather than up or straight out, and this gives him better control and balance. The effect of height is increased by the slight slope of the front face of the base (which happened to be that of the piece of walnut from which he was made). However, his arm is not fully extended, but in process of the throw, which makes the statuette a bit more compact and the arm less vulnerable. Thor's hammer is modified from a gold-and-silver depiction in an East Gotland museum; that one had a silver-braided thong, which I suggested with a short length of small-diameter silver chain glued into holes in the haft. I also simplified the design somewhat, so the hammer wouldn't be more elaborate than Thor himself. The chain adds a movable element and a bit of color contrast, as do the brass studs in the helmet and belt.

The helmet is a combination of an old Scandinavian design, with short horns added at the sides because so many depictions of Scandinavian warriors and Vikings show the horns. Most modern depictions of such horns exaggerate their length and size, and the double curvature presents some cross-grain carving problems. The completed long horns will inevitably be fragile, and fragile projections have a way of catching dust cloths and passing sleeves, or even an incautious hand. In some cases, absolute authenticity may be prudently sacrificed for permanence.

Fig. 85. (top left) The figure was blanked without power, with straight saw cuts first, followed by thinning where possible and some coping-saw shaping. Legs are drawn right and left initially, to avoid roughing blunders.

Fig. 86. (above) As waste is removed, guidelines are replaced to prevent over-cutting in any area. In this pose, the upraised arm is vulnerable and must be treated with care. Next step will be to thin body and legs to rough width.

Fig. 87. (left) Upper body and head are formed first, for proportion and to retain strength in lower areas as long as possible. Areas of upraised arm are coped where possible to avoid stress cracks.

Fig. 88. (top left) Head and arms are detailed to some degree before legs are separated. Removal of waste wood at sides of legs and through-drilling between them permit either coping-saw or chisel shaping of the leg silhouettes.

Fig. 89. (above) Details of musculature and shaping of extremities are the final steps in carving. Note that helmet horns are carved close in to avoid breakage. Figure is nude, as early Scandinavians fought.

Fig. 90. (left) Hammer and belt decorations are completed, chain added to hammer handle, and studs inserted. Studs are cut slightly over required length, then filed to a mushroom-shaped top and glued in holes.

77

Fig. 91. (top left) Hair flows in a ripple over shoulders and is delineated with veiner cuts as are beard and moustache. Ankles are thinned to proper proportion and figure is spray-varnished, with particular attention to metal to avoid tarnishing.

Fig. 92. (above) The knife was used for details, but provides a size comparison here.

Fig. 93. (left) Tilted view shows stern look of face, enhanced by drilling holes for eye pupils. Clenched-forward fist also suggests tension. Note felt rectangle glued under base—an inexpensive touch that enhances marketability.

CHAPTER XIII

Atlas – A Nude in Stress

Musculature is vital in this cramped figure

WHEN JUPITER AND HIS BROTHERS ROSE UP against their father, Saturn, and overthrew him, the Titans, a race of giants, were on the wrong side. Therefore, Atlas, a Titan leader who surpassed all men in bulk, was condemned to support the heavens on his shoulders forevermore, or so goes the Greek myth. But Atlas also grew fabulous golden apples, so Hercules took over the support job on one occasion while Atlas picked him some apples, and on another, Perseus came for some. When Atlas refused him, Perseus showed him the Gorgon head, which he was still carrying, and Atlas turned to stone, becoming the present Mount Atlas in Greece. The myths fail to explain how Atlas tended his orchard, and they mix Perseus and Hercules, but no matter— truth is stranger than fiction anyway.

I found this nude male to be much more difficult than the female ones. After all, if a female has enough softly rounded curves and is overlarge of bust and buttocks, that is acceptable, but a male must show muscles, particularly a male in the strained position of Atlas, and muscle bulges change radically with each change of pose. It is advisable to have at hand some standard text on anatomy and/or a compendium of a science-fiction illustrator like Frank Frazetta, or any reliable source in which muscles are delineated. The familiar statue of Atlas in Naples shows him as a somewhat streamlined figure, not at all bulky, and with no strain evident in muscles or face. If he is to embody the myth properly, he must be modified.

I chose walnut for the wood, partly because of its color and partly because I wanted tool marks to show, at least to a degree. They emphasize the strength and roughness of the man. I carved the figure progressively, from the top down, as the photographs illustrate (Figs. 95 to 105), to minimize the risk of breakage. Also, carving the head and arms to form helps in proportioning the lower torso and legs later. The blank can, however, be bandsawed

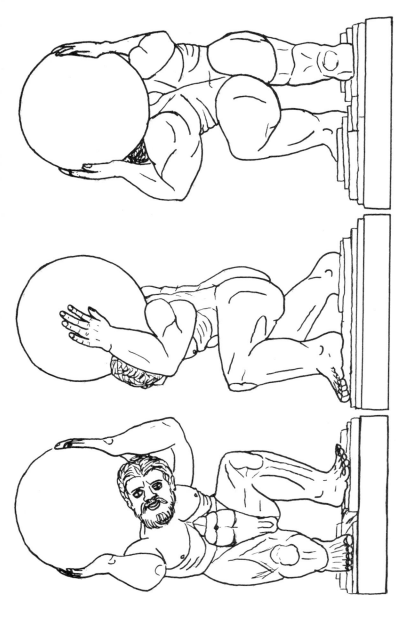

Fig. 94. Atlas is in walnut, roughly 4 × 4 × 10 in (10 × 10 × 25 cm) including base. Familiar constellations are incised on the spherical firmament, with 150 stars picked out by silver wire inserts in three diameters to correspond roughly with star magnitude (see page 85).

completely, because the wood between the legs provides the necessary early strength.

A major job with this piece is the forming of the sphere, because small inaccuracies in its roundness will be painfully evident later. Therefore, an accurate template of the desired size should be made—and used frequently. Also, frequent checks should be made to ensure that the sphere, head, and arms are in proper relationship. One tendency will be to make Atlas have an overlong neck, for example, or to give him shoulders that are too wide. Both are caused by doing too much body-shaping before the finished size of the sphere is attained, so that when the sphere is ultimately rounded, the body will no longer be in the required pressure contact. Beware if you plan to have relief elements on the sphere itself, because they may distort its shape so much that it looks grotesque. I chose the safe way and did the sphere decoration with a V-tool and knife as a final carving operation. I showed a series of constellations, each with stars indicated with silver wire. I held the figure on my knees, both to do the incising and to make the holes for the silver-wire inlay.

In any carving of this sort, it is advisable to stop periodically, as any good sculptor does, for an overall inspection. For example, on one carving I discovered I was carefully carving a six-fingered hand. Some carvings I've seen, and one which I bought, have one thumb on the wrong side of a hand. Your eye will pick up such errors if you give it the chance. Beware of concentrating too long on one little area.

When this figure was completed, I felt that the base surface should suggest a rocky area, so several parts of the surface were layered like shale. Also, the original base seemed to be too thin for the subject—size had been dictated by the wood available. Thus, another section of walnut was added to increase overall height from 8 to 10 in (20 to 25 cm).

The blank was held in a wood vise for the heavier shaping, most of it done with ½-in (12.7-cm) flat gouge and firmer, and with a light mallet. Details of face and musculature were done with smaller chisels and finally with a knife. A statuette of this size is small enough to be held in the hand for finishing, and can be turned readily for comparative viewing during the course of the carving, so it presents relatively few problems, except for those involved with depicting stress in muscles and face.

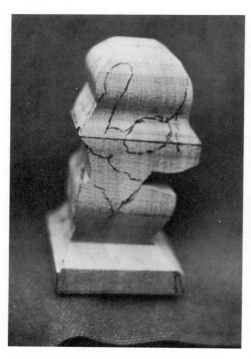

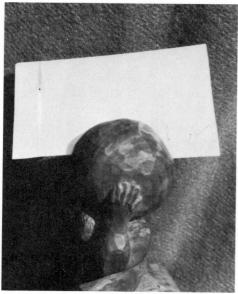

Fig. 95. *(top left) Because the figure is small, the blank can be sawed on a bandsaw. Sawed-off pieces are replaced temporarily to avoid destroying sawing guides. If necessary, they can be held in place with glue or with toothpicks in holes drilled in waste wood.*

Fig. 96. *(above) Relationship of head, neck, arms and hands is crucial, so it is best to begin final shaping with them. Avoid making the neck too long and the shoulders too thick.*

Fig. 97. *(left) If the firmament is to be spherical, it is advisable to make a cardboard template of the desired size and to use it frequently. One side of the template should be cut away at an angle from the end of the arc to provide clearance for checking near shoulders and head.*

Fig. 98. (top left) With head, shoulders and arms shaped, the torso can now be defined. Legs are not separated, however, until all heavy cutting is done; nor are feet detailed. This avoids danger of splitting near base from stress at the top.

Fig. 99. (above) Back and front of figure must obviously be worked together to be sure the torso is in proportion. Here again, templates may make frequent replacement of cutaway lines unnecessary.

Fig. 100. (left) With upper portions of figure defined, the legs can be separated and shaped. Base is lowered to reveal the feet and permit shaping of ankles. If sex organs are to be shown, wood must be left for them.

Fig. 101. (top left) Shaping of shoulder and buttock muscle bulges is important in achieving general body contours. Points of elbows and knees are formed and wrist and ankle bones located as well.

Fig. 102. (above) When contouring is complete, musculature can be put in as well as final details of face and extremities. Base has been slabbed and figure given a preliminary varnish coat to check light effects.

Fig. 103. (left) Musculature is as important in back as it is in front. Note difference in buttock heights, and stress lines in thigh muscles. Detail of base slabbing is also evident.

Fig. 104. (left) Right-side view again shows heavy thighs and legs as well as shoulders. The hands are not particularly stressed; they are merely balancing a load pressing down on shoulders and body. Fig. 105. Star holes were drilled and plugs of silver wire driven in, glued, then filed smooth. About 150 stars are shown, in three wire diameters.

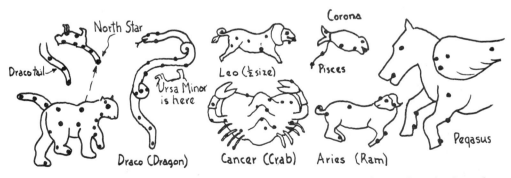

Fig. 106. Constellations were selected largely to fit the surface, though they do include the Pole Star and immediately surrounding figures in proper relationship.

CHAPTER XIV

Heracles vs. the Nemean Lion

HERACLES (Hercules in the more familiar Latinized form) was the ancient Greek embodiment of man's constant struggle against death, which was typified, for example, by his twelve labors. The son of Alcmena by Zeus (Jupiter), he was half man, half god, and the epitome of mortal strength. As Hera (Juno) was always hostile to Zeus' offspring by mortal mothers, she swindled Heracles out of his kingdom before his birth, sent two great snakes into his crib, which he strangled bare-handed, and forced the young man to submit to the master Eurystheus, who assigned him twelve supposedly impossible labors, each of which was expected to result in his death. The first of these was to slay the monster lion which was terrorizing the valley of Nemea. The lion was impervious to Heracles' club and arrows, so he eventually threw it onto its back and strangled it. One story has it that he carried the dead lion back to Eurystheus on his shoulders, so terrifying his master that he was ordered thereafter to report his exploits outside of town. In any case, he flayed the lion's skin with its own claws and thereafter wore the skin over his shoulders.

This carving, much more complex that the two preceding ones, depicts Heracles about to throw the lion. He has his right hand at the monster's throat and is stepping forward to throw him. The lion's efforts have thrown him off balance. Both Heracles and the lion are shown with tremendous shoulder development, and the lion has an abnormally large head and a magnificent curly mane as well. My drawing just fitted the available 4 × 7 × 9½-in (10 × 18 × 24-cm) walnut block so I decided to carve him that size and to provide a separate base. On this kind of carving, interior elements are very difficult to reach, so larger size increases tool clearance. However, making the carving without a base increases the problems of holding it for roughing, as well as the danger of splitting, so it is advisable to start at the top and retain the solid base as long as possible. As will be noted in Figs.

110 and 111, this was done in this case, and after the wood was removed around the legs, the hips were left square to provide an auxiliary surface for clamping while the legs were formed. This can all be done by whittling, of course, but wood can be removed much faster with the carving chisels.

It is advisable, fairly early in developing a carving like this, to bring some area to size, so the rest of the carving can be made to scale. I used the heads for this purpose. Also, no drawing I prepare can consider all the problems of conversion into three dimensions—which is why traditional sculptors make so many detail sketches. Therefore, leave wood in areas you're doubtful about so you can modify the design if necessary. I changed such elements as the pose of the lion's right forepaw and Heracles' right leg to get greater tension in the composition. The drawing must always be considered as a guide, not a

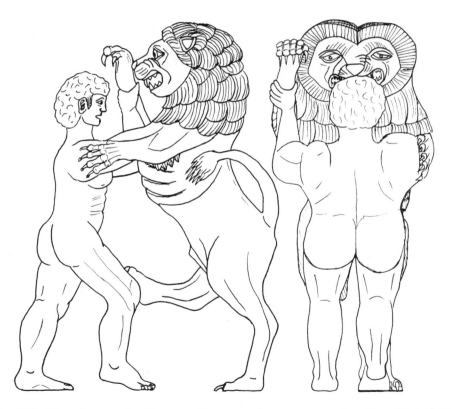

Fig. 107. Heracles vs. the Nemean Lion, a walnut statuette 4 × 7 × 10 in (11 × 18 × 24 cm) tall, including base.

Fig. 108. (top left) In the absence of a bandsaw, straight cuts were made with carpenter's saws, then sections were shaped with gouges. Interior openings were drilled through and then chiselled to shape.

Fig. 109. (above) Heads are rough-shaped and arm positions roughly defined. Because lower bodies are approximately ½ in (12.7 mm) narrower than shoulders, this wood is later removed.

Fig. 110. (left) Upper-body major lines are now defined so arm positions can be established. Clearances between upper limbs are quite close.

Fig. 111. (top left) Heads and upper limbs are carved in detail. During this work, piece is held in a vise at hips—left blocky for this purpose.

Fig. 112. (above) Lower bodies are freed and lion's mane detailed. As much waste as possible is removed with hips held in vise, using saws and chisels.

Fig. 113. (left) Rejoined figures are tested on base. Musculature has been put in, claws and eyes detailed. Figures will be pinned and glued to base at points of contact.

pattern. Furthermore, a lion's anatomy includes a somewhat triangular chest and narrow foreshoulders, four main claws, and a vestigial dew claw on each foot. His anatomy is not like a man's, obviously, so study the anatomy of animal subjects as carefully as you do those of a man or woman, and remember that there are frequently visible differences between the sexes. A book such as "Animal Drawing & Painting," by Walter J. Wilwerding (Dover #T1716), will be helpful in this respect, as will pictures of the particular animal in various poses. It is one thing to make a general static pose of an animal, another to show it under stress.

One more generality about this kind of carving: if you have no bandsaw available, make as many blocking-out cuts as possible with regular saws and remove what wood you can before using the coping saw, which is inevitably slow and laborious. Thus I cut away slabs at the sides of the carving below the shoulders, incidentally salvaging two nice ½-in (12.7-mm) slabs of walnut, as well as blocks around the legs.

The 4-in (10-cm) walnut available for the figure was too short to include the base—which made leg carving considerably easier and even helped in face carving, as we shall see. Because profile outlines of the pair are fairly vertical, this figure was roughed from the solid, except that the area from feet to hips, which is about ½ in (12.7 cm) narrower on each side than the spread elbows (see Fig. 109), was sawed off to provide some ½-in (12.7-cm) walnut for other uses. Note that the leg outlines were immediately sketched in again and that the upper portions of the piece are carved first, so that the solid leg section can be preserved for clamping the work.

I carved both heads in some detail to establish the scale for the shoulder width and the rest of the figures, then worked out the arm and hand details. When the legs were separated, I found an incipient stress crack where Heracles' right arm enters the lion's mane, and I was experiencing real difficulty in getting at the two faces as well. This reminded me of an old trick in sculpture (which would never be countenanced by a whittler); I broke the figures apart at the arms, finished the faces and body fronts properly, then glued the assembly back together—which also repaired the incipient crack. Because the lion's mane was textured, I decided not to define Heracles' hair. It was also possible to give the lion's mouth a sneer. Musculature on both figures was adapted from anatomy texts, and finish was oil and wax. Figures were pinned and glued to the base at the three points of contact, and the upper surface of the base was left smooth and untextured.

CHAPTER XV

Beowulf vs. Grendel

A statuette with close contact of figures

"BEOWULF" IS THE OLDEST ENGLISH EPIC POEM, and probably one of the oldest in any Teutonic language. It tells of the exploits of a legendary hero who went to Denmark or Norway to prove himself at the court of King Hrothulf (Hrofkraki). The king's hall was invaded each night by a fiend named Grendel who, on the night before Beowulf arrived, defeated and devoured 15 warriors and carried off another 15. Weapons were of no use against Grendel, so Beowulf, the strongest of men, decided to wrestle him barehanded. In the fight, Beowulf eventually wrenched off Grendel's arm, and the fiend crept back to his lair where he bled to death. His dam took over terrorizing the king's hall, so Beowulf went on to fight her in her cave beneath the sea, and he ultimately found and brought Grendel's head back to the king.

A gruesome tale, this one dates back to before the Saxons came to England, and we have a version dating from the 8th century. There are no depictions, either painting or statue, of the battle that I could find, so I had to design from scratch. It seemed a bit incongruous to pit a mere man, no matter how strong, against a fiend capable of carrying off 15 men, so I had to assume that there was the usual post-victory embroidery in the tale. Furthermore, not even the strongest of mortal men could tear a fiend's arm off without help, so I provided some by having Grendel gripping Beowulf's hair to push him off, while Beowulf got both hands on Grendel's arm and pushed as well with a foot in his groin.

The design was difficult, but far less so than the carving, because the combatants are quite close together, and their arms so close that shaping one may remove wood needed for the other. Then there's Beowulf's knee in the middle of everything as well. I unwittingly provided extra hazards by giving Beowulf long hair to be gripped and stacking his armor in the "blank spot"

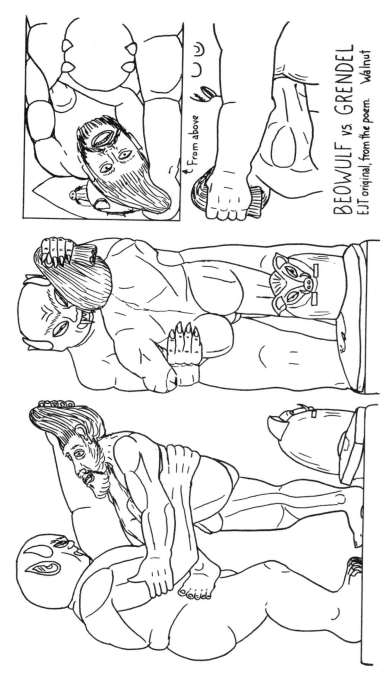

BEOWULF vs. GRENDEL

EJT original, from the poem.   Walnut

← From above

Fig. 114. Beowulf fighting Grendel, a 4¼ × 7 × 11½-in (11 × 18 × 29-cm) walnut statuette, depicts a traditional battle from the English epic. Man vs. fiend, bare-handed, provides an opportunity for intricate carving of male nudes.

behind him, so it was constantly in the way of carving the lower leg. Also, his body had to be twisted to show that his right arm would soon be in position to tug, and his face had to be distorted as a result of the pull on his hair. All in all, this was one of the most complex carvings I've ever undertaken.

The pictures show the step-by-step evolution of the figures (Figs. 115 to 126). I have included the rough drawings to show the changes that were necessary as I worked. Grendel became much heavier and amorphous, and I stood him solidly on both feet, instead of his having one foot raised. The original pose looked more like dance than battle. The available space and working room made carving of the arms and body fronts very difficult, and made it necessary as well to have Beowulf's right hand groping under Grendel's chest rather than on his arm. (It is extremely important in figure carving to check the comparative lengths of arms and legs constantly, to be certain that one limb isn't foreshortened or overextended; also, it helps to consult a good anatomy book.)

Grendel's fiendishness is suggested (I hope) by his pointed ears, small horns, fangs, and slanted and slit eyes, as well as by his gross body. Also, by leaving him big but relatively unshaped, while Beowulf's musculature is evident, he does not dominate the carving as he might otherwise. He must be far bigger and heavier than Beowulf, so Beowulf must be more defined to compensate. Everything possible must be done to show straining muscles and combat. Also, Beowulf is on one leg and is presumably somewhat balanced despite his pose, so the right foot must be centered under his body rather than being at the side. Grendel's claws could be extremely fragile if they were free, so one hand is in Beowulf's hair and the other attempting to hold him on one side, requiring suitable indentations in Beowulf's hair and flesh. Actually, the only really fragile elements in the carving are the boar's tusks on the shield, which are carved separately and inserted (with spares provided as insurance against the dust cloth). The helmet is a relatively crude "can," as it was after the Romans left, and the shield is thick because it was probably hide over hardwood, rather than steel.

The finished carving was *not* sanded, just oiled, then waxed, preserving the glow left by the tools. The top of the base was finished by scalloping with a flat gouge.

Fig. 115. (above left) Waste wood of outer silhouette is sawed away and carving begun with block clamped in a woodworking vise. Roughing starts at top of figure. Wood at lower right is left for helmet and shield.

Fig. 116. (above) With heads and shoulders separated, area between legs is drilled and chiselled out; helmet and shield positions are defined. Saw cuts define top of base on three sides and waste is cleared from below Beowulf's left buttock.

Fig. 117. (left) Shaping of the torsos is begun. This must be done carefully to avoid over-cutting. Gouges of relatively flat sweep are used with the mallet for most of this work, with care taken not to split off vital cross-grain areas.

Fig. 118. (above left) Placement of arms in confined area between figures is intricate, so is begun early. Grendel's arm must pass between Beowulf's shoulder and neck, and Beowulf's right arm must cross between their bodies.

Fig. 119. (above) Placement of arms continues, including shaping of Beowulf's left buttock so knee height and its location between the figures and arms can be determined. Also, Grendel's face is being formed.

Fig. 120. (left) Contrast between human and fiendish faces is heightened by giving the fiend a pug nose, fangs, horns, pointed ears and slanted eyes.

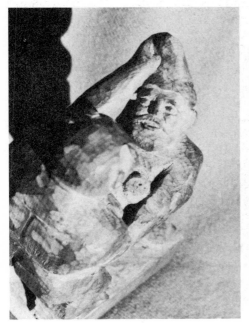

Fig. 121. (above left) Beowulf has a conventional face under stress: eyebrows pulled up, mouth open. Note knee top.

Fig. 122. (above) With head and arm positions established, hand locations and details can be worked out and arms and legs shaped. The fiend should appear to be forcing Beowulf's head back while pulling his left buttock forward.

Fig. 123. (left) Separation is cut between fiend's legs and relationship of arms worked out. General shape and decoration of helmet is determined so Beowulf's right leg can be cleared and shaped. Foot should center under body.

Fig. 124. (above left) Final shaping is completed and musculature lines added. Beowulf's physique is detailed more than that of the paunchy fiend, so the smaller figure shares the observer's attention.

Fig. 125. (above) Veiner lines are cut to establish muscle positions and will later be rounded smooth. Wrists, anklebones, fingers and toes are detailed, the fiend's with claws rather than conventional nails.

Fig. 126. (left) Boar's head decorates helmet and is repeated in low relief on shield, under which is Beowulf's sword —requiring tilting of the shield. Beowulf's hair is veiner-detailed and musculature faired-in.

CHAPTER XVI

Odysseus vs. the Cyclops – An Assembly

MOST COMPLEX OF THE CLASSICAL STATUETTES I've made, the confrontation between Odysseus (Ulysses) and Polyphemus, a Cyclops, illustrates several additional points in design and carving. It is not one piece, but an assembly of several. The two small figures are individual carvings (Fig. 127), as is the spear in the hand of one of them. The giant figure is built up as well, the arms giving the necessary shoulder width while saving wood thickness by almost half, reducing carving time and cost, and making it possible to alter arm position in final assembly. Even the base is in two sections of 1-in (2.5-cm) walnut, one across-grain of the other to combat any tendency to warp, utilizing wood that had a beveled edge—the natural surface of the trunk from which the plank was cut. Incidentally, the added base-piece made it possible to pose the spearthrower more accurately and dominantly.

Assembling a carving has a number of advantages: It permits last-minute adjustments, such as the proper contact between the giant's foot and Odysseus, makes full carving of the small figures relatively easy, permits insertion of the soldier's arm in the giant's hand so that he appears to be squirming, and the like. In a solid carving, all of these decisions must be made in the original design and wood must be allowed for them thereafter. Also, sawing and carving are complex because of obstructions and grain problems. If the carving is commissioned, carving in parts saves time and wood—and the client's money. Overall effect is not harmed, and only the careful observer will note that the work is not a single unit.

The original Greek myth had it that Odysseus and his men were captured on their way home from Troy by Polyphemus, chief of the Cyclopes, the one-eyed giants. Polyphemus imprisoned the Greeks in his cave, closed nightly by a huge boulder which he rolled before the opening. This was opened each day to allow his sheep out to graze, but was far too heavy for Odysseus and his men to move, so killing the Cyclops sentry was no solution. However, the giant was dining on one man a day, so Odysseus encouraged Polyphemus to overdrink, then put an eye out with a heated stick while Polyphemus was in a drunken stupor. When Polyphemus rolled the stone back to summon help, Odysseus and his remaining men clung to the wool under the sheeps' bellies and passed under Polyphemus' questing hand undetected.

But this client wanted more action and was willing to vary from the myth under the usual explanation of "artistic license." In any case of man versus giant, the ostensible hero is dwarfed. To counter this to some degree at least, I gave Odysseus a breastplate and greaves which were slightly whitened (pigment rubbed in and wiped off), the only "color" on the carving, so that the observer's eye would be attracted to the smaller figure.

The Cyclops is about to push Odysseus over with a contemptuous kick. This adds action, difficult in such carvings because of the diminutive size. Figures in a composition should not just pose; rather, they should be under stress, suggesting that some action is taking place, or about to take place. The carving should, in effect, tell a story. Initially, the angle of Odysseus' spear was not exactly correct (if the Cyclops' eye is the target) and I didn't want solid contact between the figures (which would throw off Odysseus' cast), so poses could be adjusted during assembly.

Note that the Cyclops' feet are in line with each other and with the center of his body. This is important. When a man stands on one foot, his body shifts sidewise to center over the support, and even the upraised foot will tend to center as a result. Note also that Odysseus' left arm is not extended straight forward but slightly to the right; this again is natural. Also, his left foot is forward to balance his throwing arm and give maximum force to the throw.

Polyphemus' single eye can be a problem. It is centered in the brow, but does it protrude or is it recessed as ours are? What happens to the facial areas occupied by our eyes? What of the point where eye and nose meet? Obviously, the eye is not shaped, but symmetrical, and normal eye sockets must not even be suggested although the cheek shape must be retained. I decided to bulge the eye and use what would normally be eyebrows to provide an under-emphasis, leaving a flat area below them that rounded up into the cheek; the nose is normal, as is the hairline, when this is done.

There are no particular problems in carving these figures. The two small ones, which are only about 3 in (7.5 cm) high, are easy, except for Odysseus' strained-backward position. The other figure can be carved with his arms in any desired position because the arm will be cut through at the elbow anyway to allow his upper arm to go in one side of the hole in the giant's hand while

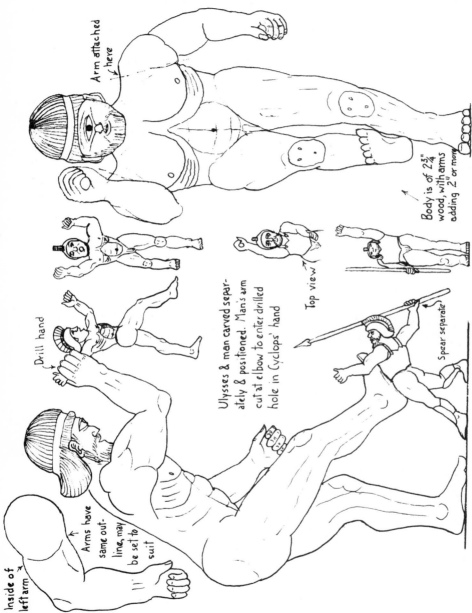

Inside of left arm

Arms have same outline, may be set to suit

Drill hand

Arm attached here

Body is of 2¾" wood, with arms adding 2" or more

Ulysses & man carved separately & positioned. Man's arm cut at elbow to enter drilled hole in Cyclops' hand

Top view

Spear separate

Fig. 127. Ulysses fighting Polyphemus is a statuette in walnut about 6 × 8 × 10½ in (15 × 20 × 27 cm). The giant's arms, the two smaller figures and the base are separate pieces.

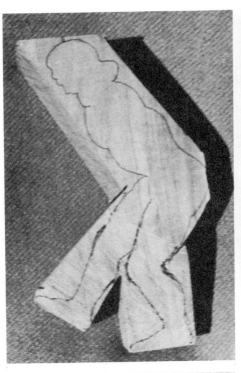

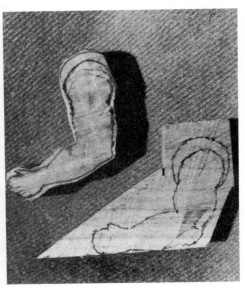

Fig. 128. (above left) Assuming no bandsaw is available, the Cyclops body is blanked from 4-in (10-cm) walnut by straight saw cuts. Grain is vertical (as seen) to add strength to supporting left leg.

Fig. 129. (above) Arms are duplicate silhouettes, cut from the triangle of waste wood behind head. They are cut individually from half-thickness pieces; or, they may be bandsawed and then separated. Note added wood at shoulders.

Fig. 130. (left) Ulysses and his soldier are whittled from smaller pieces of walnut. Each is about 3 in (8 cm) high. Ulysses has white-tinted breastplate and greaves, as well as inserted spear. One arm of the soldier will be cut for insertion.

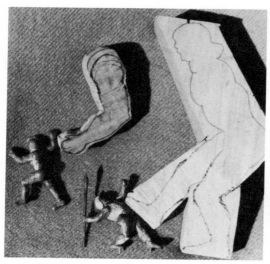

Fig. 131. (above left) Small figures provide scale and pose for the larger one. They should be compared frequently. Note that Ulysses' feet are given mounting pins before final foot shaping, to avoid breakage. Fig. 132. (above) Roughing-in of Cyclops' body and arms is done simultaneously to assure correct proportions. Right leg crosses body to center the foot. Left fist is tightly closed, right fist more open to hold soldier. Fig. 133 (far left) Face modelling is complicated by single central eye above the bridge of the nose and the forward bend. Eye was made slightly oversize and pupil drilled to accent it. Hair is banded. Note torso musculature. Fig. 134. (near left) Muscles are delineated also on back and lower legs. Buttock shapes are varied because of lifted right leg. Hair is formed to a flared bob in back, and delineated by veiner cuts.

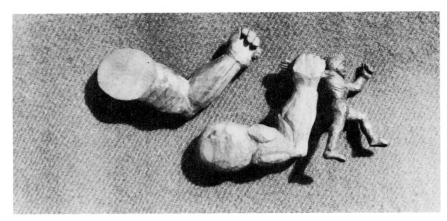

Fig. 135. *Arms are muscled and tentative assembly of right arm made with shoulder. Then arms are tested with Cyclops figure to get best positions and to taper joining planes at shoulders. Shoulders are still oversize.*

Fig. 136. *(left) When poses of arms are decided upon, arms are glued in place and pinned with cut-off brads through drilled holes. Shoulders are brought down to size and faired into body. Fig. 137. (right) The planned base was a section of 1-in (25.4-mm) walnut with one edge tapered as it came from the tree. It seemed better to place Ulysses on a slight rise, both to reduce foot contact with Cyclops and to aim spear, so a cross-grain block was added.*

his forearm goes in the other. It is obvious that Odysseus' feet should be flat on the bottom to provide secure mounting. I increase security of such mounts by inserting a steel pin made from a finishing nail in each, and the same for the giant. These supplement gluing. A pin could also be used between Odysseus' chest and the giant's toe, but a spot of glue is probably enough.

Because the arms are made separately, they can be set wide at the elbows to make Polyphemus appear very brawny and wide. This is done by sloping the shoulder pads on the arms and on the body as well. Both sets of shoulder pads should, by the way, be cut too large initially and not cut to size until the arms are applied, so the pectoral and deltoid muscles can be faired in as they should be. I made the arms alike in silhouette, so they could be sawed together from the scrap triangle behind the head of the Cyclops, then cut into two half-thickness sections. (Allow extra wood around the hands also, because the right fist must be larger than the left to allow for gripping the Greek soldier.) And don't forget that the arms are a pair—a right and a left —and carve them accordingly.

After the arms and body are rough-shaped, cut through the arm of the Greek soldier and insert the parts, then try the giant's arms in various positions. (Note that I drew them in one position and placed them slightly differently—Figs. 127 and 136.) Check the bevels on the shoulder pads to be sure they are flat and mate properly, remembering that there are natural clefts at the inner edge of the pectoral and deltoid muscles which can mask the joining line. The shoulders for a burly person should be about three head-widths, so the space from head to bevel on the body and bevel to outer edge of the shoulder should each be about half a head. This can, of course, be adjusted after assembly, but it is preferable to get them approximately right beforehand.

When you are satisfied with the arm poses, make sure that you've done what carving you can in the tight area under the arms, then glue and pin the arms in place. Be certain that the arms are neither too high nor too low on the body, and that the right arm is slightly higher than the left, because the arm is raised, bulging the pectoral and deltoid muscles on that side. Final forming of the arms and shoulders can then be done (be sure to have a good anatomy text at hand).

On a composition such as this one, I find that a combination of carving with chisels for the heavy cuts and whittling the details is fastest and easiest. Small gouges and veiners are, of course, essential in putting in hair, shaping eyes and ears and the like.

CHAPTER XVII

Elfish – a Whimsy in Wood

A case study in design

THE LITTLE PEOPLE—ELVES, DWARVES, FAIRIES—and flowers have always been associated in my mind; there is something supernatural about flowers, and the Little People are pastoral—the inventions of rural imaginations. This book is evidence of that fact. Thus, when it came time to plan an appropriate cover for this book, I conjured up the idea of an elf fishing in a lily. (Goblins, fairies and dwarves are all too big, and gnomes are too fat.) My flower guide further informed me that only the wood lilies (and the tame variations of the Easter or Bermuda lily) open upward; the others open sideways or down. But the wood lily's six petals narrow at their bases to form an open basket rather than a tulip-like cup, and there are no visible sepals. The stem is long and weak. So I decided to use my artistic license and design a lily with a solid cup and sepals and with a short stem, if any at all.

The elf was to be big-eared, with a slant-eyed, puckish face and "harum-scarum" hair. Where was he to sit? On an adjacent toadstool? On a rock? Why not on a petal of the lily itself? Should he be napping, alive, fighting a fish? I tried the latter two in sketches, and selected the one with the bite. My first pose suggested too small a fish, so I redrew the elf leaning back and with arms straining out and down. What of stem, leaves, lily size, base? Should it be in the round or in relief? The latter is obviously easier in this case, considering pole, line, pistils, petals and other fragile elements. But 3D would be more graphic and challenging. Size should permit detail on the elf, so I selected a 7-in (17.5-cm) diameter for the lily corolla. I had a trunk of walnut and a block of dense mahogany with an angled grain. Because the wood lily is orange-red, I chose the mahogany; and I opted for building up, rather than one-piece carving.

I detail all this because it suggests the processes involved in arriving at an idea for a minor sculpture, none of them really involved with carving, except

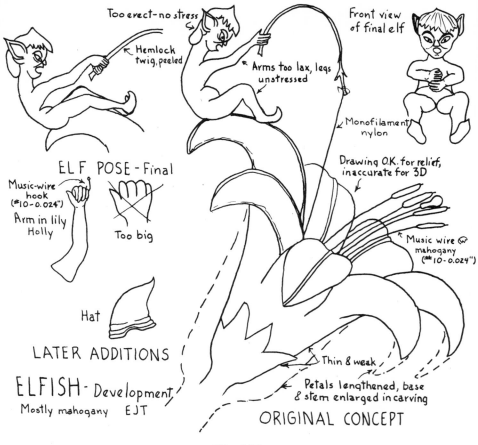

Too erect-no stress

← Hemlock
twig, peeled

Front view
of final elf

← Arms too lax, legs
unstressed

← Monofilament
nylon

Drawing O.K. for relief,
inaccurate for 3D

ELF POSE - Final

Music-wire
hook
(#10-0.024")

Arm in lily
Holly

Too big

← Music wire @
mahogany
(#10-0.024")

Hat

LATER ADDITIONS

ELFISH - Development
Mostly mahogany   EJT

↙ Thin & weak

← Petals lengthened, base
& stem enlarged in carving

ORIGINAL CONCEPT

Fig. 138.

possibly the decision to carve in the round and to build up instead of making
a monolith. There were still many decisions to be made, but they could be
postponed: stamen and pistils, water level inside, fish showing or not, exact
location and pose of elf on a petal, even the angle of flower and base. This is
a virtue of built-up construction, as is the fact that some contrast can be
attained in color of elements, as well as their workability. Also, such elements
as the pole and line and the pistils can be made of more practical materials
and the elf and lily can be carved with grain suiting the design—and fragility
is vastly reduced.

As the design worked itself out, I found that the lily was by far the most
difficult part; it took at least three times as long as the elf. So I have provided
step-by-step pictures of carving the lily.

Elfish—An elf fishing in a lily has a surprise bite

(**Fig. 139**) The lily has fragile petals and stem, and thus should be carved to a plan that provides a method for holding it. My mahogany block was 11 in (28 cm) long, so it provided a good clamping base. I sawed in from all four sides to the diameter of the lily corolla—3¼ in (8 cm)—about ½ in (12.7 mm) under the ends of the petals, and the same distance at the base of the flower. Wood was cut out with a heavy chisel and the resulting central pillar was rounded roughly. Then I rounded the top into a rough 7-in (18-cm) circle and laid out the six petal areas. A ½ -in (12.7-mm) core hole was then drilled and the hollowing begun.

(**Fig. 140**) A short trial showed that undercutting beneath the petal tips—removal of a "doughnut" of wood over 1 in (2.5 cm) thick and about 6 in (15 cm) in diameter—would be time-consuming, but that the process could be speeded up considerably by cutting out wedges to separate the leaves and thus providing some saw clearance inside the petal. Gouges could then be used with less fear of breakout, and the petal edges could be thinned. (It is necessary to work from both sides of each petal to avoid splitting out part

Fig. 139.

Fig. 140.

Fig. 141.

Fig. 142.

of the petal at the top of the "U" that it forms.) The block can be clamped upside down in a wood vise if the petals are left rough-shaped.

(**Fig. 141**) When undercutting is completed, the petals can be shaped. These should vary slightly in shape and width, with varying petal curvature as well. Actually, some may be carved to slightly overlap others. Veining is done by carving lines with a veiner to create a central rib, then removing the wood at each side to form a ridge. The ridge should be rounded on top and tapered in width toward the point of the petal. On the inside of the corolla, the veins can be extended down a short distance and then faded out.

(**Fig. 142**) There should be a water level inside the lily, which means that you must select the angle at which the flower is to be mounted as well as that of the petals. Remember that one petal must be higher than the others to support the elf. Here the "water level" can be seen, as well as a core hole above it. I decided at this point to replace the expected fish or splash in the water with a ghostly hand reaching up to hold the line, so I provided a core hole for it. The water surface is in miniature waves, and the petals are shaped down to meet it.

(**Fig. 143**) Rather than the plain basket-like base of a real lily, I decided to add a ring of sepals, so I cut them in as I narrowed the base. It also seemed advisable not to have the flower without a stem so, when the bottom of the cup was formed, I cut away the base to leave one. If carved according to scale, the stem would be too fragile—even though grain runs vertical. My original thought was to drill the flower base for a dowel, but having an integral stem made it possible to have a slight curve and some desirable irregularities in it.

(**Fig. 144**) A lily has six stamens—in this flower, like miniature cattails—and a pistil resembling an inverted flask. Stamens were drilled in mahogany (first!) for #10 music wire, then whittled to shape, as was the larger-diameter pistil. All were glued to wires, which were inserted into drilled holes in the "water level". They were assumed to be hanging downward (to the right in photo), to clear the upper area for the miniature ghostly hand.

(**Fig. 145**) A hand carved in mahogany proved to be much too large, so a much smaller hand and arm were carved in holly, so it would stand out against the mahogany surrounding it. The elf was blanked out of mahogany, but of a lighter-colored, coarser-grained variety than the lily for a slight tonal contrast. Note the hand positions, to grip the fishpole, and the exaggerated ears of the elf. He is to be without the normal cap, which was made separately and mounted lower down on the petal to suggest that it had fallen off. These pieces were whittled.

(**Fig. 146**) The arm was glued into the core hole, then surrounded by glue-drenched mahogany dust to fill in any gaps around it. A miniature fishhook made of music wire is held easily in the little finger—as though all of the elf's efforts are negligible. The elf was positioned on the petal with pins made from finishing nails and glued in place, his lost hat glued and pinned below him on the petal. The fishpole is a branch of hemlock, skinned and bent while green so it would dry into position. The base was a half-log of *guachepil*, the Mexican name for a solid, strong wood used in ships and resembling locust, but with more variety in color. I used it as a base because it is heavy and I had a piece with the bark still on, resembling a sylvan setting. Finish was varnish and wax.

Fig. 144.

Fig. 143.

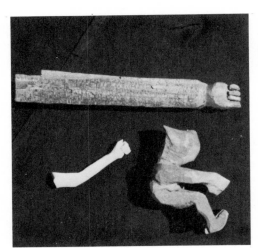

Fig. 145.

Fig. 146.

CHAPTER XVIII

The Unicorn – Lady's Choice

How to adapt a design as you carve

THE UNICORN HAS ALWAYS BEEN POPULAR, probably because of the well-known legend which claims that when it meets a virgin, it will put its head in her lap and become tame and powerless. It has also become associated with power, purity, spiritual force and divine creativity. It is used to symbolize the Incarnation (thus to represent or symbolize Jesus), and the presence of the Word of God in the Virgin Mary. It is depicted in the famous French tapestry, the Virgin and the Unicorn, as well as in others.

The unicorn (or *monoceros*) is an excellent example of how myths are born. The ancestors of the Vikings had the boats and the nerve to hunt in northern waters far from land, and they encountered narwhal herds. They

Fig. 147.

carried the tusks home, and some tusks found their way into central Europe through trade. But the Norsemen either didn't tell the origin of the tusks, or created the legend. Gradually, a complete myth was built up about the animal and the horn, and it became a popular medieval symbol. The story grew that the horn came from a creature described as essentially a horse with antelope legs and cloven hooves, a tail like a lion, and a goatee, plus a very luxuriant mane. The horn was of varied length, but twisted upon itself (as is that of the narwhal), and was considered to have magical powers in medicine and aphrodisiacs. Royal jewelry, sceptres, even thrones, were fashioned from it, and pieces were ground into a very marketable powder to be added to potions.

The unicorn was depicted in various works of art, including tapestries, and was incorporated in the British royal coat of arms. Popular playing cards depicted a wild man, or hairy man of the forest, riding a unicorn, thus combining two legends. The myth was brought to America and carried over into our folk art and tales as late as the last century—and is used in popular designs even today.

Like the legend of the biblical flood, unicorns also appear in the literature of other cultures. A unicorn-like animal, more leonine but with a single horn and its ruff forming an aureole around its head, occurs in Chinese folklore, notably the Chi-Lin. It was supposed to appear only at the birth of a great sage.

When I was commissioned to carve a small unicorn, my client and I agreed upon a *couchant* pose (lying down with the head raised). Preferably, the figure was to be carved in a light-colored wood, with the head turned back rather than an action pose (see Fig. 147). I selected Port Orford cedar, partly because I had a block of it that measured 3½ × 6 × 10½ in (9 × 15 × 26.5 cm) and was relatively free of visible knots. I planned on a separate and contrasting horn and a luxuriant mane. The front legs would be side by side, and the animal would appear to be resting on a ledge. This would permit a base that could be clamped during carving. So much for sketches and planning! As it turned out, the block tapered from 3¾ in (9.5 cm) to 3½ in (9 cm), from one end to the other, and was short of the height needed for the head.

Carving the Unicorn—step by step

(**Fig. 148**) The sketch was transferred to the block and the block was rough-sawed to silhouette. The slab that was cut away from the back was glued at the head to increase the height there to 7½ in (19 cm). Wood was chiseled away behind the head and the back and tail areas, then the rounded-mane shape was scroll-sawed. It immediately became obvious that the centerline of the mane had to be a spiral to meet the back at the foreshoulders, and that the animal had to lie on its far side if the forelegs were to be side by side. If the body was to be relatively vertical, the forequarters had to be twisted forward, or the legs—at least the right foreleg—had to extend towards the front rather than being brought to the left.

(**Fig. 149**) It seemed advisable to shape the head first and to resolve the body pose thereafter, because the nose had to be at the front of the block to allow sufficient depth for the rest of the figure. Therefore, the head was rough-formed with a ¾-in (19-mm) flat gouge, the neck curve worked out, and the front line of the shoulders established. The head was sawed to approximate thickness and taper, so ear positions could be established as well. It turned out that a knot ran exactly through the center of the goatee, so this was left attached to the body wood of the shoulder as long as possible to support it.

(**Fig. 150**) About this time, it became apparent that the head pose was complex, so it was worked out in detail, including the mane, neck garland, throat, and ear and horn locations. Reference to horse photographs gave head details but no example of a head turned back. I remembered two sets of Chinese horses I had, each with one horse with its head reversed. Neither turned out to be particularly helpful, because the Chinese had simply swiveled the head 180°, and in the case of the ivory head, the carver had depicted the mane running straight down so it ended between the forelegs! Also, I wanted to avoid a prosaic, flat base, and to suggest instead a sylvan ledge. I had already tilted the sketch on the block to make the base thicker at the front of the animal.

(**Fig. 151**) A reasonable spiral for the centerline of the mane was drawn, and a technique for the mane worked out—primarily large curls at both sides of the centerline and in an irregular pattern. Also, the body was to lie vertical, with the right foreshoulder somewhat advanced, as it would be naturally, and the right leg, even though tucked under the chest, would of necessity not cross as far as I had originally drawn it. The new position was easy to estimate by using the dimensions of the visible left foreleg as a guide.

(**Figs. 152 and 153**) Once these decisions were made, blocking out of the rest

Fig. 148.

Fig. 149.

115

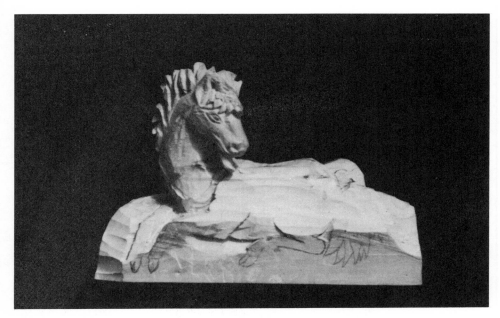

Fig. 150.

Fig. 151.

Fig. 152.

Fig. 153.

117

Fig. 154.

of the figure was relatively easy. The tail was carved, and the legs defined.
The base was rounded to make the hooves stand out, and textured with a flat
gouge. The neck decoration, instead of being a simulation of a decorated
leather collar, was made to resemble woven miniature flowers, with a heart
hanging over the breastbone. For the horn, an available scrap of walrus tusk
was ground into a spiral shape, then sanded and scraped to a dull sheen.
Fortunately, the ivory had a slight curve, which helps the effect. The entire
piece was sprayed with three coats of matte varnish, then the neck garland
and areas of the belly and under the legs were tinted slightly darker, and,
finally, the whole piece was waxed.

APPENDIX

"Proper" Size and How to Attain It. Finish. Sharpening.

What size should a carving be?

IN MOST CASES; THERE IS NO REAL REASON why a carving must be of a particular size, unless it is part of an assembly. Size is usually dictated by other factors, like the available wood, convenience in carving, or the size of the tools available. A miniature can be harder to carve than a larger piece, simply because your tools are too large, or the amount of detail you plan to include is too great for the grain or texture of the wood. Further, a miniature is hard and dangerous to handle, as well as fragile. Similarly, a piece that is overly large adds to the problems of handling and removal of excess wood— you may find it difficult to hold the work as well as find a place to display it when completed.

The patterns in my books can be enlarged as desired by any of the several methods described herein; only in rare instances is it practical to reduce size and retain all the detail shown. As a general rule, it is advisable to reduce, rather than increase, detail; it is a tendency, particularly for whittlers, to include so much detail that it tends to overpower the subject itself. What you are seeking is an image of a bear, not a texture that suggests a bearskin coat; or a rhinoceros, not a complex pattern of plates and wrinkles. A carving should be readily identifiable, unless you intend it as a puzzle. If a portrait of a person includes too much prominent detail, we are immediately conscious of it, because we are accustomed to the soft curves in the faces and figures of people we know, not hard lines. A sculptor uses a live model or good pictures of his subject; even a tyro must do the same if his design is to be believable. You must do your homework!

So: Be sure you haven't selected a size that has details too small for your tools, or your skill, and that it does not include elements that your hand, and

119

your eye, cannot execute. Be sure that the wood you have chosen is sufficiently dense and fine-grained for the detail you plan to include, and that the grain is not so prominent that it will overpower the detail, or distort the appearance of the entire design; and, at least initially, don't make the piece so big that it is hard to handle or requires excessive waste removal before you can actually carve. Particularly in 3D carving, you may have to spend half your time getting unwanted wood out of the way before you can begin the interesting part of the work—the actual shaping of the form. I must, in all fairness, point out that the more nearly the design fits the available wood, the less waste you have to remove (and, in a sense, the less wood you waste). Also, if you plan to sell the carving, a larger carving generally commands a higher price, even though it may require less work. This thinking even affects inexperienced carvers, who will quote a lower price for a work of smaller size—and find to their chagrin that the time and effort involved are much the same.

How to make the subject fit the wood

Very often, the drawing or photo you want to use as a design is the wrong size—usually too small. If you can get a negative, a photographer can enlarge or reduce a print to suit, or if there is a nearby art studio with a photostat machine, they can do the job. This will provide a silhouette, which is often all you need.

The Pantograph, a device something like that used to maintain contact with the overhead line on an electric train, is now becoming readily available. It can be set for various ratios. There are also proportioning dividers and calipers, the pivot of which can be adjusted so you can measure a dimension on the original with one end and get an enlarged or reduced measurement on the other end. These are particularly useful in sculpture, where guidelines are difficult to retain anyway. You can make your own calipers or dividers; they're simply an X-shape. If the pivot is placed so arms on one side are twice as long as those on the other, it will provide two-to-one enlargement or reduction. Obviously, such a tool has limited range, so that you may need several of various sizes.

If you have none of these recourses, don't worry. You can make a simple elastic band enlarger, as shown in Figure 156, which will give you an outline for the blank, which is often all you need. If you don't have an elastic band long enough to cover sketch and wood when lightly stretched, link several together. You anchor the band with a thumbtack or pin at one end, and put

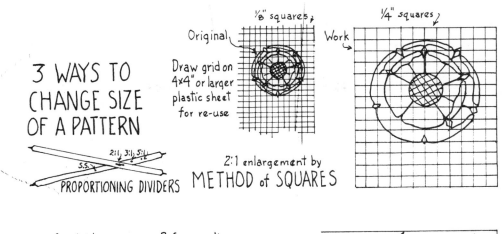

3 WAYS TO CHANGE SIZE OF A PATTERN

PROPORTIONING DIVIDERS — 2:1, 3:1, 5:1 — S.S.

Original, Draw grid on 4×4" or larger plastic sheet for re-use — ⅛" squares

Work — ¼" squares

2:1 enlargement by METHOD of SQUARES

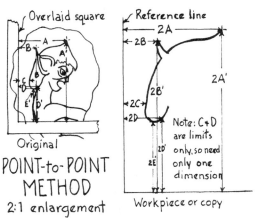

Overlaid square

POINT-to-POINT METHOD
2:1 enlargement

Original

Reference line
2A
2B
2A'
2B'
2C
2D
Note: C+D are limits only, so need only one dimension
2D'
2E
Workpiece or copy

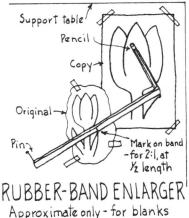

Support table
Pencil
Copy
Original
Pin
Mark on band -for 2:1, at ½ length

RUBBER-BAND ENLARGER
Approximate only - for blanks

Fig. 156.

a pencil in the other. Put an ink mark along the band to correspond with the enlargement you plan: a third of the way for 3:1, halfway for 2:1, and so on. As long as you keep the band stretched a bit and the pencil square, you can enlarge anything fairly accurately.

The traditional method of enlarging is by the method of squares. Draw a grid of ⅛-in (3-mm) squares on transparent paper or plastic (you can save it for re-use) and lay it over the original. For 2:1 enlargement, draw a grid of ¼-in (6-mm) squares on copy paper or directly on the wood. Then copy the original square by square, as sketched (Fig. 155). For 3:1, the grid on

121

the work should be ⅜-in (9-mm) squares, for 4:1, ½-in (12-mm) squares, and so on.

The third method, which I use quite frequently in laying out sketches from a photograph or clipping, is the point-to-point. Make a basic square of cardboard or paper, and fasten it to the original with transparent tape so that it touches, or nearly so, two of the sides of the subject. Draw a pair of lines at right angles on the copy sheet or workpiece, and transfer dimensions of prominent points, in each case multiplying the original dimension by the scale. Thus, if the horizontal distance is ⅜ in (9 mm), and the vertical distance 1 in (25 mm) on the original, and you are doubling the size, the point you locate on the copy should be ¾ in (18 mm) horizontally from the side line and 2 in (5 cm) from the bottom line. When enough points are located, you draw connecting lines, much as a child does on those number puzzles in the Sunday supplement. This is slow, but very accurate, for complex designs—at least for me, because simple arithmetic is my dish.

How shall I finish my piece?

Finishing is so much a matter of the individual carving and of personal preference that it is difficult to lay down even a general rule. Thus, I have indicated throughout this book what finish was used, whenever I knew or could determine it.

If a piece is made in soft wood and painted, I prefer to see the color applied thin and wiped down somewhat, so that the wood shows through in flat areas while the color accents lines and depressions. I use oil pigments thinned with flat varnish or drier, but acrylics can be thinned and used the same way. Heavy painting creates a shiny, plastic effect and denies the handwork and the wood.

It is also possible to dye or stain soft-wood pieces; I have done both with good results. I recently dyed the small birds of a mobile with cloth dye, in the absence of anything better; the colors were vivid, at least. I also have a series of German sal-ammonia-based stains called "Beiz," developed especially for woods. They include a wax, so color and polish are applied in a single operation, as with some American oil-and-wax stains. With the latter, and contrary to instructions on the can, it is usually preferable to give the piece a coat or two of matte (satin) spray varnish before staining; this prevents the stain from oversoaking into end grain and causing an over-emphasis there.

For hardwood carvings, I prefer not to use fillers or much of the other paraphernalia and procedures of cabinetmaking, unless the carving is part of a piece of furniture and must have a similar high gloss. There are two schools of thought on this subject, and many variations between. Some sculptors like a high gloss on their work, so they sand and polish and fill and varnish or shellac, just as furniture makers do. The opposite school, of which I am a member, uses sandpaper, but sparingly if at all, preferring to let the tool marks show. Also, the wood is left without fillers or coloring, unless it be antiquing for depth, and is finished with flat varnish and wax, oil and wax, or wax only, depending on wood and subject.

How to sharpen tools

The edge of a tool—any tool—is like a saw under the microscope, with teeth projecting at various angles, and feathery filaments projecting from them. The sharper the edge, the fewer the feathers and the smaller and better aligned the teeth. Using the edge misaligns the teeth and blunts them, so constant resharpening is necessary.

There are four steps to sharpening. grinding, whetting, honing and stropping. Grinding is the first and coarsest step and is rarely necessary, except on tools that have been nicked or broken or resharpened so often that the edge is blunt. Grinding was once done on a grindstone, which moved at a slow speed, but is now done on a high-speed wheel, so the danger of burning the tool edge is everpresent. If the wheel surface is loaded—filled with grains of soft metal or wood or even pencil lead—or the tool edge is not kept cool, there is danger of burning the thin edge. This draws the temper, evidenced by blue, brown or purple discoloration, and makes the metal soft so it will not hold an edge. Thus, you should never grind a tool unless it is absolutely essential and unless you know how, and then you should cool the tip twice as often as you consider necessary.

The next two operations, whetting and honing, are also grinding operations, but with progressively finer-grained stones. They are usually done by hand. Whetting is done on "Washita," a yellowish or grayish natural stone; honing on "Arkansas," a white, very hard, uniform and fine-grained white stone. ("Arkansas" is also the material for "slips," the small shaped stones used to take the feather edge off the inside of gouges and V-tools.) There are now manufactured stones available for both of these operations. Some have whetting grain on one face, honing grain on the other. In day-to-day carving, honing is frequent, whetting much less so unless the wood being carved is particularly hard or abrasive.

The final operation is stropping, which is what a barber does to a straight

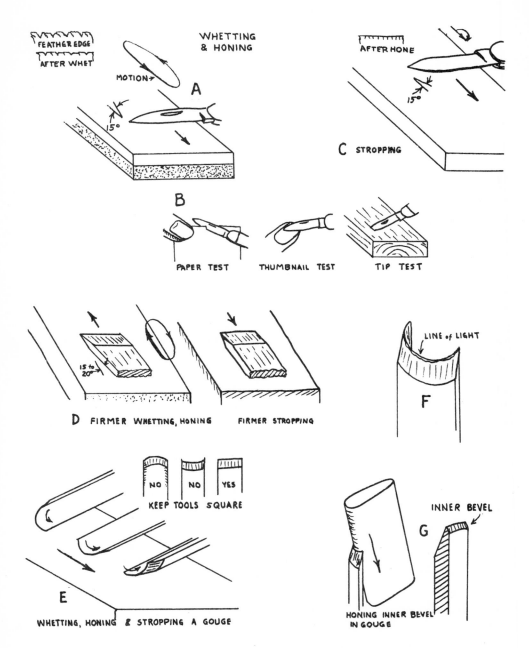

WHETTING & HONING

FEATHER EDGE
AFTER WHET

MOTION

A

15°

AFTER HONE

C STROPPING

15°

B

PAPER TEST   THUMBNAIL TEST   TIP TEST

15 to 20°

D FIRMER WHETTING, HONING   FIRMER STROPPING

LINE of LIGHT

F

NO   NO   YES
KEEP TOOLS SQUARE

E WHETTING, HONING & STROPPING A GOUGE

INNER BEVEL

G

HONING INNER BEVEL IN GOUGE

Fig. 157.

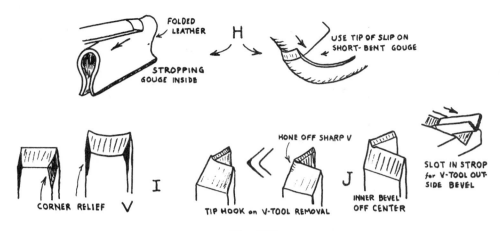

Fig. 158.

razor. It essentially consists of stroking the edge on leather to align the tiny teeth, and produces an ultra-sharp edge like that of a straight razor.

The typical tool nowadays is sold ground and whetted. It is quite sharp to the touch, but requires honing and stropping before use. Knives are ground so that the blade itself has the proper included angle, and require only a "touch-up" for sharpening. A properly ground firmer has an included angle of about 30°—15° each side of center—and the center line of the tip should be that of the tool also. Gouges have the same included angle, but it is all ground on the outside of the tool—the concave inner surface should be flat.

Some carvers prefer a hollow-ground edge, one that is slightly concave, usually from the peripheral shape of the wheel which grinds them. (The hollow-ground shape is exaggerated in a straight razor.) Hollow grinding makes initial whetting and honing easier because the angle just behind the cutting edge is less than it should be, reducing drag behind the cutting edge, and is claimed to make the tool stay sharp longer. This is true when cutting soft woods, but the edge may turn or nick on hardwoods or imperfections.

I have tried to sketch the motions used in sharpening tools (Fig. 157), both to maintain their edges and to insure uniform wear on the stone. Many stones become channelled through excessive wear in the middle, and this results in dullness in the center of the cutting edge of a firmer, and in rounding of the outer corners. (All operations on stones are done by pushing the edge toward the wheel or stone, while honing is done by passing the heel over the strop first.) The stone should be kept lubricated with thin machine oil, or even with a 50-50 mixture of machine oil and kerosene, and should be wiped off and replaced when it turns gray from included metal particles. Also, the stone should be washed with benzine or gasoline periodically, or boiled in water containing a little baking soda. This lifts out soaked-in oil and grit. If you have manufactured stones, just heat them in an oven and wipe them off.

To sharpen a knife, I use a rotary or figure-8 motion (Fig. 157 *A*) bearing down a bit harder as the edge is moving forward and slightly lifting the handle part of the time to be sure I touch up the tip. Unless the knife is very dull, a few swirls on whetstone and hone, in turn, should do it. Sharpness can be tested by trying the edge on a fingernail or on paper—it should "stick" on the former and slice the latter when drawn across (*B*). This operation will also detect any nicks or dull areas. Then the knife is drawn for a stroke or two over each side of the strop (*C*)—which is usually a piece of thin plywood with rough leather glued on one side, smooth on the other. The rough leather is impregnated with oil and crocus powder, while the smooth side has oil only. Stropping is done with the blade heel-first; you can speed the operation by rolling the blade over the heel at the end of a stroke and reversing direction. Incidentally, it is good practice to learn to strop a tool almost absent-mindedly, so you can plan the next cut as you do it.

Carving tools are sharpened in much the same manner, particularly the firmer (*D*). However, the sharpening of gouges is a bit more tricky. The tool must be rotated slightly as it passes over the stone, so the entire edge is treated (*E*), and too much roll means rounded corners while too little means dull corners that will tear the wood rather than cutting it. Dullness on the edge may be seen as a line of light (*F*). Also, because all sharpening is done from one side, a wire edge forms on the inside; it can be felt as a tiny burr with a fingernail. Thus the final operation in honing a gouge is to pass a slip down inside to take off the wire edge, and to do the same thing with a piece of leather in stropping. I have sketched the method (*G, H*). Some carvers thin the edge of chisels behind the cutting edge to relieve drag (*I*).

The parting or V-tool is a special problem to sharpen, because there is a tendency for a tit to form at the tip (*J*), or for the sides to slope back. This must be guarded against at all costs, and it may be advisable to whet or hone away just a very little of the bottom of the "V" at the tip so the cutting edge there is no thicker than it is at the sides.

Many carvers hate sharpening and try to avoid it by every possible means, including disposable blades. Some have devised methods of regrinding in fixtures on belt sanders, and whetting and honing in a single operation on buffing wheels, even grinding and whetting gouges on shaped wheels as the manufacturers do. But for most of us, hand methods work best because the frequency really isn't as great as it seems.

The carver who sharpens his own tools soon learns to treat the edges with care, both in use and in storage. Tools should be placed side by side on a bench or workplace, with their sharp ends toward you so you can pick out what you want rapidly and surely. They should be stored in slots so the edges don't touch, and when carried about should be in a portable carrier or in a canvas or other roll that protects the ends. Also, before you begin to carve, it is advisable to strop and probably to hone each tool; some professionals I know, like barbers, strop a tool each time before they use it, and have hone and strop readily accessible, as much in evidence as the tools they service.

Index